HOW WILL OUR CHILDREN SURVIVE?

Brian J. Noble

But wherefore do you not a mightier way
Make war upon this bloody tyrant time?
O let my books be then the eloquence
And dumb presagers of my speaking breast

WILLIAM SHAKESPEARE. SONNET 16 & 23

INTRODUCTION

Whatever you might think about this book, or about me, I can assure you I am not a doom and gloom merchant. I'm actually quite upbeat. I like socialising and parties and dancing the night away, and am a definite Billy Connolly fan. But sometimes, just sometimes, when the world is taking on the distinct shape of a pear, things have to be said. So I'm going to say them: no-matter how unpalatable, no-matter how grotesque. In view of that let's get on with it, because what follows might just be the un-declared 'Third Secret of Fatima.'

I'm sure you've noticed. This world has become a running sewer, made that way by man. Man in the form of corporate companies. Man in the form of governments, or men in the form of entire countries with their nonsensical concerns about Gross Domestic Product, as if consuming ever more and more is the answer to the world's problems, when in fact the complete opposite is true

The world is no longer a pretty place: not with us in it. There are of course exceptions to the rule, such as the occasional exceptional people, like Bill and Melinda Gates, who, along with their new 'Goalkeepers' initiative, have probably done more to ensure improvements in health, education and the reduction of poverty, than any two individuals that have ever lived. Plus the *very occasional* company, such as Lego, that recently contributed $100 million to the children of the Rohingya camps in Bangladesh: including initiatives by the United Nations and several struggling NGOs, and Christian groups, endeavouring like the Titanic deck-crew to lower the boats before the ship actually sinks.

Problem is, the iceberg struck so long ago, and with such force, recovery is in serious doubt, and may never happen. Not with the current lack of international altruism. Not with the concept of expanding consumption as the route to happiness. Not with this level of hate and despair and violence and personal concern for a seat in the lifeboat.

Humans have an absolute catalogue of bad habits, including the fact that we routinely ignore evidence we dislike. Such as the American Second Amendment, which has gun crime in places like Milwaukee County in Wisconsin, utterly out of control, and yet they have recently made weapons easier to buy and to carry. In total thirty-one states are 'open carry states' meaning anyone can walk around fully-armed, like Wyatt Earp. What do they expect to happen?

We consistently rationalise our biases inventing justifications for horrendous decisions; such as the one above.

Everyone awake; everyone not actually dead, hears the cry... Don't let me drown, Oh Lord! Not me. Not the CEO of such a major company. Not me either: such a well known senior politician. And definitely not me: a top of the tree police officer. And certainly not me: a well known NHS surgeon. And of course not I, such an exemplary and well known Christian bishop. And please God not us. Not an ordinary Joe or Jane that nobody's ever heard of, and of which none of this is our fault.

No one wants to drown - but we are all drowning: drowning in sorrow at our pathetic attempts to live comfortably, securely and happily on this benighted planet with its manifold problems.

Let's face it: even though in the last two or three hundred years humans have made staggering scientific progress, this planet doesn't want us! It certainly doesn't need us and would be tons better off without us. But by a remarkable set of astonishing and unlikely accidents (or God created circumstances) we are here. We are still walking the decks of the sinking ship, deciding how much extra weight it needs to finally founder and desperately trying to make the pumps work harder while kidding ourselves that we can cope. We have it under control – of course we do – anything else is surely "fake news". We will be saved. By who, or what exactly, is not specified.

For some, it's a greater and yet greater understanding of the laws of science. For others it's a universal omnipotent God. For yet others it's simply the saving grace of market forces, and for others still, it's a given political agenda, or a given individual: a saviour, such as a returning Jesus.

But a combination of common sense and clearly unobtainable theism tells me there isn't a saviour! There isn't going to be a re-emerging miraculous Jesus – and we would need ten thousand couples like Bill and Melinda Gates and ten thousand companies like Lego. There is (as it happens) a given international polit-ical agenda, but no-one seems to be listening, and there is (since the final demise of the Industrial Revolution), no longer a viable and sustainable market force that makes any sense.

And if there is (or once was) a God: a cosmic consciousness, some scientifically unknown but suspected force in the uni-verse aware of our existence and concerned for our welfare, he either abandoned us a long time ago, has fallen asleep, is running a hologram for his own amusement, or is now dead – or sadly, never existed in the first place.

Either way, we're on our own. And this time, we cannot shake hands with the devil and walk past him. We have to face him – head-on, and resolve the world's problems by our own efforts, and we all know what we have to do. We have, of course, to stop warring with each other which will immediately reduce a large measure of world poverty. We have to stop thinking *our* religion is better, truer, more Godly than *your* religion. We have to stop nationalism and nationalist thinking, in which my country is better, bigger, smarter, and more deserving of the planets riches than yours.

We have to stop rampant runaway capitalism in which the only concern is profit occasioned by more and more unnecessary consumption. (*Did you know that British merchant banks are awash with Russian mafia blood money? And did you know that the eight richest people's wealth equals the poorest 3.5 billion?*). Plus, we need to reign in rampant nonsensical personalisation, in which the only ambition is fame. (*When asked, eight out ten teenagers declared that their greatest wish was to achieve fame.*)

We have to consistently denounce and remove dictatorial regimes everywhere (but not by force). We have to face the facts of global warming and do radical things to alter it. (*The latest IPCC report says we have twelve years in which to save the world.*) We have to understand the destructive power of the drug trade: including the legal, the barely legal and the strictly illegal, and stop it. We also know we have to seriously limit, or completely do away with nuclear weapons as part and parcel of a peaceful non-warring world, and we must stop using plastic which is adding to the demise of the planet.

But above all!

We have to face the unpalatable fact that *all* the still usable fossil fuels will completely run out within thirty-five years (or less) meaning of course that, well before then, the price will be catastrophic. If the world is unprepared, chaos and death will follow like a pet Velociraptor.

We must do all of these things, and as quickly as possible. The Intergovernmental Panel on Climate Change (IPCC), insists we must break our addiction to fossil fuels, eating meat, flying in planes, and all, and every other form of reckless consumption in general: *right now!* But above all, we must confront the head-in-the-sand denial that has prevented us from making changes that should have been made yonks ago. And we have to do all this immediately (*New Scientist* 8 December, 2018. p32).

But will we?

NO, OF COURSE WE WON'T! – AND YOU KNOW DAMN WELL WE WON'T!

At least, that is to say, we won't do all of them. We may be able to scrape around the edges of some of them. The plastic problem: we might eventually resolve. The meat problem: *very difficult,* we need to overcome the powerful lobbies involved. The antibiotic problem: only if government money intercedes. The global warming problem: *just maybe*, if we can limit the warming to 1.5°C above pre-industrial levels, and eliminate the cretin Trump and people who think like him from the equation. But since several oil companies are still searching and sometimes finding, yet more oil, this seems ever more unlikely.

Rampant, blind, capitalism, in which producing more and more goods in an attempt to make more and more consumers spend more and more money, might be reined in, when its obvious shortcomings start to evacuate its bowels over everybody. The Mexican stand-off currently inherent in Britain's Brexit, might eventually resolve itself peacefully. There are glimmers of hope... As I write this on New Year's Day 2019, they are merely glimmers. But generally speaking, greed (particularly corporate greed) poverty, the drug epidemic, religious fervour, political controversy and war, will either take thousands of years to resolve, or will never be resolved. Maybe that's what the 'Fermi Paradox' is telling us. It's not that they were not out there. It's that they couldn't maintain being out there. So what can be done? Where can we go? How can we survive? But strictly speaking, since all these problems hover on the horizon like a chained rabid dog, just out of our reach, the question should be: what can our children and our children's children do to survive all or any of this?

CHAPTER 1

"What can be predicted with absolute certainty is that the decline is coming and our oil consuming world is grossly unprepared for it. Somebody needs to get busy writing the script for act two."

Mathew R. Simmons, energy advisor to George W. Bush and member of the National Petroleum Council

The human condition is such that, according to anthropologists, we fared much better in small groups of fifty to a hundred, as was once the case several thousand years ago, than we do as civilised humans in our dirty, overcrowded cities and latterly xenophobic nations.

Animal studies do not always translate to humans, but in certain cases an analogy can be, and has been drawn. Rats in close confinement become psychotic and bullies always emerge. Similar experiments by the Nazis discovered the same result with their human guinea pigs. This helps to explain how they managed to herd Jews and Gypsies into concentration camps. It probably could not have occurred, were it not for the natural animal thanatophobia which appears to be part of our heritage.

But our crowded cities, with their constant battles against grime, crime, and corruption, are not the biggest problem facing humankind. Nor is it the big corporations and *their* manifold corruptions, some of which are examined in this book. And neither is it the worldwide plastic pollution problem that is slowly destroying the entire eco-system and has long ago entered the food chain. And although frightening to contemplate, it is not the unfortunate rise of antibiotic-resistant bacteria. Nor is it the coming lack of drinkable water across huge swaths of the planet.

It's not even the differences between Muslims within Islam, caused by the non-acceptance of Abu Bakr by the Shia, leading to hundreds of thousands of pointless deaths. Neither is it the un-founded Christian belief in their religious superiority over every other religion, furthered by the Western – specifically, American – governments' belief they have a God-given right to control us all. Nor is it the tragedy of a thousand child victims of predatory priests in Boston USA, or even the sure and certain knowledge that all of cult Christendom is awash with such paedophiles.

And believe it or not, it's *not* global warming, though that is a very, very serious issue, and even though Mark Watts, the executive director of C40 Cities has said that,

> "Without urgent action people in cities everywhere, particularly on the coasts, will be subject to catastrophic flooding, heat waves, serious food and water shortages, and electrical blackouts lasting weeks: all within your child's life time."

Neither is it war, or the perennial fear of nuclear annihilation – even though President Obama once tried to instigate an international ban on nuclear weapons, and all three branches of the federal government, Legislative, Executive and Judicial, ignored him – because what controls them is the industrial military complex and their overriding concern is profit.

It's not even Trump's ludicrous abandonment of the hard-won non-proliferation treaty. It's the totally unrecognised by-most-people fact that, within your child's lifetime **both oil and gas will completely run out and sufficient replacement energies do not** *exist now and will not exist then!*

And no matter what you have been told by Fox News, the BBC, the printed press, oil companies and oil economists, or anyone else: there is no viable substitute for oil or gas on the horizon, or even close to the horizon. And the overall life of oil and gas is not seventy years, or fifty years –it is *thirty-five* or considerably less (some experts say two decades less). Such a catastrophic loss of oil and gas will mean a worldwide energy loss, and an energy loss of that magnitude means never before witnessed international price rises, leading to worldwide chaos, worldwide starvation, and millions of deaths. Even in the so-called developed world. But we can't wait that long. Kevin Anderson of the Tyndall Centre for Climate Change Research in the UK, has said,

> "To even come close to the Paris target of 2°C the use of natural gas must be entirely ditched across the European Union by around 2035, an urgent programme to phase out existing natural gas and other fossil fuels is imperative."

That's seventeen years!

You have doubts about the entire zeitgeist? About the alarmingly short timescale involved in running out of fossil fuels and the urgent need to stop using them long before they are exhausted anyway? I don't blame you. So did I... Until, as an investigative journalist, I started doing some serious research into this subject, and the results are frightening. They are not just another hackneyed conspiracy theory. They are not fake news. They are very real.

Read on....

*

You have noticed that your boss is often or almost invariably wrong. The organisation you work for is not up to scratch, is inefficient. There are far better ways to do the job and you can clearly see them. So can I, and (believe it or not) so can your boss, and your compatriots. So can anybody, anywhere: but things don't change.

The political party you represent has taken and is still taking a wrong course: the ministry you work for (and not just the Home Office) is 'not fit for purpose' and probably never will be. All the other politicians can see it and are fully aware of it. You are aware that they are aware: but nothing really changes.

The new product you are attempting to make an industry believe in is obviously far more efficient than the methods they currently use. They know it, everyone concerned knows it: yet they still ignore you.

The operation you just had went wrong; you lay there sensing it had gone wrong. The pain was intense. They gave you aspirin. 'We don't do things wrong', they said. Later they found a swab in your belly. No apologies, no recriminations. 'A minor human error', they said: 'happens all the time', they said: 'get with the programme' they said.

The car you had transmission problems with and collected last week for a kings' ransom and an assurance she was perfect, is running badly again. In fact, the automatic box is jumping gears. 'Bring it back', they said. You took it back. 'It's not the same problem', they said. 'That problem's been dealt with. This problem has been caused by the previous problem which of course we fixed. This problem will only cost you three times what the previous problem cost.' Two weeks later it's running rough again.

In short: human beings are not just fallible, not just cock-up artists magnifique. They are covetous of the facts, protective of their own interests, concerned with their own infallibility and, on many occasions, outright liars. The consequence is that very little changes and when it does, it has all too often been thought through by an aide to an aide with a master's degree in obfuscation.

So understand that, whenever any government or government department, which is composed of several outright liars and many obfuscation and cock-up artists, tells you that something is going very well, it's probably going very badly. When you are told that the Dow Jones is going to affect you personally and everyone's life is going to improve, it isn't (it only tracks thirty companies anyway). When you are told there are weapons of mass destruction, there aren't. When you are told that 9/11 was caused by Iraq and so we have to invade it, it wasn't (it was caused by Saudi Arabia). When you are told that climate change is a myth, it isn't. When you are told that the rule of law is simply being applied to bring about a democratic solution to an unhappy situation, not initially of their making – it simply isn't true.

So – and this is one of the major points of this all-encompassing harangue – when you are told that the oil in the ground will last for at least another fifty or a hundred years (or even, as one Oxford economist has it, forever) and in the meantime tar-sand oils, tight oils (such as shale oil or fracked oils) and bio-oils of various types will stretch that possibility even further, and there is nothing at all to worry about, because alternatives will be found in time, they are exaggerating, obfuscating, confounding the issue, to the extent that they are outright liars. And if you are reading this while still in the industry you must know that, too.

Of course, the bosses of the oil industry have their own interests at heart and agree with governments who take their advice from free market economists, who are violently opposed to economic models that are not based on continual growth. However, just as described in the first paragraph, the majority of people (at the top) who work in the industry can see the failures and understand the faults. And the major fault is not the threat of spilling the damned stuff. The major fault is that it has peaked just about everywhere, and is therefore starting to run out everywhere and – believe it or not, no matter what you have been told, or read, or seen on television – *there is no immediately available replacement for oil.*

That is, unless you want the entire northern part of the planet covered in corn or rapeseed, and the entire southern part covered in soybeans, sugarcane and palms: and, of course, windmills everywhere, as far as the eye can see. Even then, it could not possibly match the amount of energy used by 93 percent of the world's transport, let alone the world's industry. Plus, the energy used to grow such voluminous amounts of oil-producing crops would halve the energy available for use, and there would be no room left to grow food.

However, there are other possibilities that need to be explored and explored pretty damn quick, too.

Petroleum geologists and independent experts in the oil industry, when not speaking on behalf of any oil company, have their own story to tell. It's a different story from that of the oil companies, the economists, the politicians and the average press release. This story is frightening.

*

I relent just a shade from the previous rant. There are a couple of politicians I have recently spoken to, both female, who see this disparity between where we are now, in the extremely well-off, tail-end of the Industrial Revolution, with its deepfreezes, shopping malls, and television car adverts, and where we will be. Because they also realise it is coming to a sticky end and that replacement possibilities for oil and gas, while available, are a very long way off. Both these ladies are unusual because one of them, simply by chance, picked up a book entitled *The Long Emergency* and lent it to her friend.

If we do not come through with the alternatives, and the short-term oil forecasts are correct, the end will be more than just sticky, it will be catastrophic. But it might eventually resolve itself into one that will bring back local markets, where people will shop every day for perishables, where genetically modified, or the cheaper and easier CRISPR (a revolutionary genome editing technique) modified crops are once more growing in all our fields and life has stepped back a hundred years or more. Evangelicals will call these dark times 'the tribulation' but I guarantee there will be no rapture to relieve either the population pressure or graveyard real estate pressure: just ordinary starvation, misery, and finally death.

To that end, my country, the United Kingdom, should no longer be wedded to a Europe that controls every law. Brexit needs to work, for a lot more reasons than overhearing unfamiliar East European languages in the supermarket. We need to be separate, small, and as self-sufficient as possible: as self-sufficient as we were before the oil age. Even more so, because there will be no colonies to make up the shortfall.

The two Westminster politicians (who do not mind being mentioned, but do not wish to be named) have themselves realised that the general public is completely ignorant of this unalterable fact, and that the population at large does not have the first clue that they are sleepwalking into an entirely different future.

They are also aware that it's going to be particularly frightening for their children, my children – and, of course, yours too. And for our children's children, it might well be a veritable nightmare for a long, long time, comprising an entirely changed world of few citizens and no energy source worth a damn (unless we all get our act together faster than greased lightening). And almost certainly, because of politically unstoppable global warming, there will be intense heat in the summer causing widespread fires, followed by freezing winters, violent storms and constant flooding, wedded to diseases we cannot stop or even stall, such as the noxious bacterium Klebsiella, (CRKP), which has apparently mutated and is now resistant to *all* known types of antibiotics, including the last commercially available;

colistin.

These shocking, but very real races against time can be offset, can be partly cured before the snake actually strikes, but the antivenin has to be administered now – right now! Profit must no longer be a concern. The corporate world's shareholders must take a back seat and help to deliver and governments must step up to the plate – *no delay must be permitted.*

*

Dr Richard G. Miller, who worked for BP from 1985 until he retired in 2008, has said that official data from the International Energy Agency (IEA), the US Energy Information Administration (EIA), the International Monetary Fund (IMF), and other sources, showed that conventional world oil production had most likely peaked around 2007/2008.

Dr Miller explained how the official industry line, that global reserves will last fifty-three years at current rates of consumption, *is absolute nonsense*, pointing out that, "Peaking is the result of declining production rates, not declining reserves."

Despite very few new discoveries and increasing reliance on unconventional oil and gas sources, thirty-seven countries are already post-peak, and global oil production is declining at over 4 percent per year, or 99 million barrels a day: over 35 million barrels a year. Dr Miller commented that,

> "We need new production equal to a new Saudi Arabia every three to four years to maintain and grow supply. New discoveries have not matched consumption since 1986. We are drawing down on our reserves, even though reserves are apparently climbing every year. These reserves are growing due to better technology in old fields, raising the amount we can recover – but production is still falling at four point one percent per annum."

That doesn't sound all that serious, does it? But let me tell you quite plainly, it is damnably serious.

Dr Miller's job was to prepare annual projections of future oil supplies for British Petroleum from 2000 to 2007. He has referred to this as the ATM machine problem.

> "More money, but still limited daily withdrawals, production of conventional liquid oil has been flat since 2008. Growth in liquid supply since then has been largely of natural gas liquids, ethane, propane, butane, pentane and sand bitumen type oil. There is a growing consensus that the era of cheap oil has passed and that we are entering a new and very different phase. A sustained decline in global conventional production appears probable before 2030, and there is significant risk of this beginning before 2020. On current evidence the inclusion of tight oil [shale oil] resources appears unlikely to significantly affect this conclusion, partly because the resource base appears relatively modest."

It is considered by experts to be a fact that increasing dependence on shale oil (known as unconventional oil or tight oil) could actually worsen the declining rates. Per Dr Miller again,

> "Greater reliance upon tight oil resources produced using hydraulic fracturing will exacerbate any rising trend in global average decline rates, since these wells have no plateau and decline extremely fast – for example, by ninety percent or more in the first five years.

Plus, this method of extraction is desperately detrimental for the environment. It uses vast amounts of water, which is unusable afterwards because it is oily scum that is contained in huge lakes. These lakes often leak into the water table, but there is no real incentive to cure this problem, even though there are start-up companies that have discovered methods of passing electricity and sound waves through water, cleaning it to the extent that it is almost drinkable, certainly swimmable. This also applies to conventional mining tailings, but of course it costs, and so is ignored.

Dr Miller has said that,

> "The final peak is going to be decided by the price – how much can we afford to pay? If we can afford to pay $150 per barrel, we could certainly produce more given a few years of lead time for new developments, but it would break economies again."

Peak oil is the industry's way of saying 'after this point oil is declining and prices can never return to pre –2004 levels. (Oil prices increased in February 2018 from $50 to $60, and in June/July to $65 a barrel. It has since fallen again to around $55 a barrel. However the day is not too far off when it will reach $100 a barrel again, and never stop climbing. Remember, you heard it here first!).

Dr Miller continued,

> "We're like a cage of lab rats that have eaten all the cornflakes and discovered that we can eat the cardboard box too. Yes, we can; tight oil may reach five or even six million barrels a day in the US, which will hugely help the US economy *in the short term* [author's comment] along with shale gas. Shale resources, though, are inappropriate for more densely populated countries like the UK, because the industrialisation of the countryside affects far more people, who have far less access to alternative natural space, and the economic benefits available are spread more thinly across more people. Tight oil production in the US is likely to peak before 2020. There absolutely will not be enough tight oil production to replace the American current nine million barrels a day of imports."

Nevertheless, the current scuttlebutt is that a group of oil companies, including UK Oil and Gas Investments (UKOG), Cuadrilla Resources, and Angus Energy, are planning to drill thousands of new wells in English National Parks, even though a few years ago fracking was banned in all British National Parks. Clearly the companies believe they have found a legal way to bypass the original fracturing ban by using an acid rock dissolving technique.

Acid drilling has become a known method of liquefying the surrounding rock (in this case mostly limestone), rather than directly fracturing it. This method still has a substantial impact on groundwater.

The target area in question is known as the Kimmeridge, a limestone area which has been compared to the huge Bakken oil field in North Dakota. It is recorded that UKOG, the largest player in this market, is attempting to extract over a billion barrels, requiring 2,400 wells using acid drilling.

Several companies have already bought up drilling licences across the southeast of England and, according to Greenpeace, the wells will cover almost 180,000 acres of outstanding natural beauty and scientific interest.

Aside from the environmental impact, all 'tight oil' extraction is short-lived, obtrusive, unsightly, and simply pushes renewable technologies further and further into the background, when they need to be very much in the foreground.

In America, the problem with 9 million barrels of imports is that the huge oil reserves in the Middle East and elsewhere are running out. The above view was put to the *Guardian* journalist Nafeez Ahmed, in December 2013. It's now 2018 and I can assure the situation is far worse. Nafeez Ahmed has said,

> "Peak Oil as a concept applies globally, but is based on the summation of individual nations experiencing peak oil. In *State of the World 2005,* the World watch Institute, observed that oil production was in decline in thirty-three of the forty-eight largest oil-producing countries. Other countries have also passed their oil production peaks."

The following list shows some oil-producing nations and their peak oil production years. All the fields in these nations are now declining fast.

Germany 1966	Russia 1987	Oman 2000
Venezuela 1970	Egypt 1987	Norway 2000
Libya 1970	France 1988	Mexico 2003
USA 1970	Indonesia 1991	
Iran 1974	Syria 1996	
Nigeria 1979	New Zealand 1997	
Tobago 1981	UK 1999	
Peru 1982	Australia 2000	

An ABC television program which aired in 2006 predicted the following (then) future oil peaks.

- Algeria: 2012 (actually peaked 2006)
- Qatar: 2019 (actually peaked 2007)
- Angola: 2010 (actually peaked 2008)
- Azerbaijan: 2013 (actually peaked 2010)
- India: 2015 (actually peaked 2011)
- China: 2009 (actually peaked 2018)
- Iraq: 2036 (may have already peaked)
- Kazakhstan: 2020 (estimate could be much lower than claimed)
- Kuwait: 2033 (may have already peaked, according to the World Bank)

- Saudi Arabia: 2027 (could be over 40 percent lower than claimed) and experts estimate peaked at Ghawar and Safaniya in 1981. Other fields in Saudi Arabia such as Abqaiq. Zuluf, Khursaniyah, and some eight or ten others, peaked in the 1970s. The only reason the large wells haven't reached dew point (*the point at which there is insufficient pressure to keep the oil, water, and natural gas in the oil separate; causing the gas to bubble out of the oil and form a cap: effectively the end of the life of the oil well*), is because of a massive pressurized water injection programme that began decades ago, forcing the oil to the wellhead.

Canadian conventional oil production peaked in 1973, but oil sands production will continue to increase to at least 2020, when it will also peak.

They are all are emptying alarmingly fast, much faster than people realise, including the oldest and largest of the group in Saudi Arabia, the Ghawar (although Saudi Aramco, says it has oil to last ninety-years). In fact, the *Guardian* newspaper, quoting WikiLeaks, estimates a huge percentage overstatement of its recoverable reserves. Meanwhile, oil experts say, 'the ninety-year oil' claim by Aramco, is *complete and utter nonsense*, and simply Saudi government spin.

The Stanford GSB Alumni Association and the Woods Institute for the Environment calculated, in May 2018, that if we relied on individual countries to maintain the world's oil supply, Canada's oil would suffice for six and a half years: Central and South America for three years: Africa for two and a half years: Europe and the Far East combined would last three and a half years: and the Middle East – incorporating Iran, Iraq, the United Arab Republics, Saudi Arabia and Kuwait – for approximately twenty-three years, based on the current understanding of what the real amounts remaining are likely to be.

Also in May 2018, the *Insider* newspaper, quoting individual speakers from the above conference, carried a headline that the world's oil will run out in only **ten years.** Speakers commented that the latest measurements confirm that the oil is running out very, very, fast indeed – much faster than any oil company or oil executive is willing to admit – and will be absolutely gone within ten to twenty years.

To be fair to at least BP, if no other company, they are experimenting with innovative ways to recycle used engine oil using a sort of oil cartridge that will gradually supply just the required amount of oil for the engine to heat correctly. At oil changes the cartridge is removed and another inserted. The old one is kept intact and its oil cleaned. This product, the company assures me, will be available by 2020. That's a year from now. So far no garage I have spoken to, has even heard of it

BP is also manufacturing an aircraft fuel called Biojet that they sell in Scandinavia. It's a low-carbon jet fuel made from partly recycled cooking oil; this fuel is said to reduce (immediately released) greenhouse gasses by more than 60 percent. Conventional jet fuel (used just about everywhere) creates twenty-four tons of CO_2 every 1,000 miles and on an average day there are 10,000 aircraft in the air. Few travel less than a thousand miles. So if we say that 9,000 aircraft are in the air, going at least a thousand miles (many of course are going ten times that) on any given day, that amounts to a minimum of 9000 x 24 = 216,000 tons of CO_2 being pumped into the running sewer of our atmosphere every single day. Imagine the result in a month – in a year.

(New Scientist of January 2019 has the facts. Global emissions in 2017 were 859 million tons of CO_2. Jets are theoretically allowed up to 50 percent biofuel, but only 143 out of 39 million scheduled flights in 2018 used any kind of blend at all. The International Council on Clean Transportation has suggested a return to propeller aircraft ASAP. Synthetic biofuel entirely from crops has also been suggested. But to supply the present passenger need [only the present need] half the planet would be growing the appropriate crops. The estimate is that in 2017, 400 million cubic metres of fuel was used,

equivalent to 3.4 million square kilometres of oilseed rape or canola. Meanwhile one person in nine, worldwide, doesn't have enough to eat. Or if seaweed were used, it would have to be gathered in hundreds of billions of tons annually. Both are assumed by biological scientists, to be complete non-starters!)

Furthermore, what most people do not realise, is that biofuel produces just as much carbon dioxide as any other carbon based fuel, but when growing it, the plant absorbs carbon dioxide from the atmosphere. This is called being 'carbon neutral'. A lot of people think the basic thinking behind the so-called 'carbon neutral' concept is completely nonsensical, in that taking out

CO^2 with the left hand (via the plant) and placing even more CO_2 *(because of planting, harvesting, transportation, and factory reduction of the plant)* back into the atmosphere with the right hand, is ludicrous, and a totally clean none CO_2 producing method of flying aircraft is imperative. To fly an aircraft on present (or even possible future) battery technology would require, according to the University of Breda in the Netherlands, batteries larger than the aircraft itself.

Such attempts, as those by BP, to alleviate the coming nightmare are innovative. But to what extent are they simply marketing spin to make an oil company look less demonic? Katherine Mannion, British Petroleum's 'Advancing Low Carbon' programmes director, has said,

> "The world is facing a huge challenge. The global population is rising and expected to reach 9 billion by 2040. The standard of living is rising for many people who want access to transport, to nutritious and plentiful food supplies, to development and so on. But how are we collectively going to meet this massive demand while also reducing emissions?"

It's a very good question, Katherine, and while you obviously represent the best of the bad, I suggest (along with numerous oil experts) that tinkering around the edges simply won't do it. Huge, stupendous, colossal, change is necessary: plus, an immediate acceptance of that fact by the current White House administration.

Incidentally, Saudi Aramco will announce its Initial Public Offering (IPO) in late 2018, or early 2019. If you are a share-buying type of person, the argument for unlimited oil or very limited oil will make the available shares either worthwhile buying, or hardly worth buying at all, depending on who is right in this manuscript's forthcoming argument.

As a divergent view, reference investing in any kind of fossil fuel, on 12 July 2018 Ireland's parliament voted for a bill to divest itself over the next five years of the £8 billion investment in oil and gas it currently possesses. It wishes to be the first country in the world that passes a law prohibiting its government to invest in fossil fuels – ever again.

Believe it or not, there is currently no *viable* replacement for oil and gas, no matter what baloney you have heard or read in the press on the BBC, NBC, Fox News, or anywhere else for that matter.

I'm making you, the reader the jury. Until you have read this book the jury is out.

*

Most of the world's oil comes from about 900 giant oilfields (well, they were giants once) usually called 'elephants' with only a score being considered the very largest: including those in east Texas, western Siberia, and the previously truly massive Ghawar and Safaniya fields in Saudi Arabia, with about 5,000 to 7,000 or so (the actual number is secret), other smaller Saudi wells, also producing oil.

By 1985 the world had been geologically mapped, just about everywhere, in an attempt to find more of these huge freebee underground sponges (there are no lakes of oil, as in the popular mental picture, it is obtained from sedimentary rock and sand-stone acting like a sponge) *and there were none to be found.* And unless they are hiding in Antarctica or the deepest parts of the ocean where, at current prices, that oil is likely to remain, the ones we have, are the only ones we have.

The Soviet Union, unhampered by conventional business con-straints, searched every inch of Siberia and they found huge amounts of oil and gas. But they are now part of the world's understood oil and gas reserves and thus accounted for in the number of barrels left to exploit.

It was therefore made clear, before hydraulic fracturing and tar sands were discovered, that conventional crude oil well pro-duction had universally peaked in the 1960s to 1970s. Further discoveries after that were (and still are) of smaller fields which played out quickly: some in only two years.

To view any kind of peaking, you must first historically go past it, then look backwards, in a manner the oil writer James Kunstler calls, 'the rear- view mirror effect'. This showed that peak discoveries preceded peak production, by approximately thirty years.

Total world peaking of the entire global oil production oc-curred (according to a number of experts) around 2006 to 2007. Certain economists (in the pay of the oil companies) disagree and consider the situation, while very close, has not occurred yet. However, in all of this, one thing was made clear. The bulk of the world's oil was disproportionally consumed in the last fifty years – within your lifetime.

In historical terms, that's the blink of an eye.

The oil business has been traditionally prone to sudden shifts in price, occasioned sometimes by quite minor political events, at other times by major events. One such was the Shah of Persia being deposed during the Iranian revolution in 1979, a circum-stance that ushered in the mad mullahs led by Ayatollah Ruhollah Khomeini.

Revolutionary Shiite Islamic fundamentalism was born long before the Sunni version of ISIS and ISIL and a dozen others, and throughout 1979 Iran placed a stop on oil exports, supplying only its own domestic needs. Under the Shah, Iran had been the world's second largest oil exporter after Saudi Arabia, representing 5 percent of the world's oil production. The Iranian revolution sparked fears of the madness spreading to other oil-producing Islamic countries; panic buying ensued in anticipation of price increases which, in fact, caused the very price increases that followed.

Then in autumn 1979, Islamic students, high on extremist propaganda, Allah and country, attacked the American Embassy in Tehran, shouting that it was 'a nest of spies' (which it might very well have been) and took fifty-two staff members hostage. The attempted rescue operation by an American Delta Force, code named 'Eagle's Claw', went spectacularly wrong and eight servicemen died. The hostage crisis lasted over a year and put paid to the presidency of James Earl Carter. To the Iranian sky pilots, the United States was the epitome of the Great Satan forecast in the Koran, and hence caused one of the bitterest culture clashes in history, which continues to this day.

In 1980, Saddam Hussein's Iraq invaded Iran (both principally Shiite), severely damaging the Iranian oil wells and initiating a bitter eight-year conflict that removed 8 percent of the world's oil, causing the price to rise sharply again. This in turn spurred further exploration because it was now affordable to do so, which caused a glut in the market and the price fell once more. The major companies withdrew from exploration and oil cities such as Tulsa and Houston went into decline.

But lower oil prices meant rebounding economic growth rates and America, in particular, began huge suburban building programmes (a concept no longer viable or sustainable). The OPEC countries began to suffer and were forced to compromise on a stable pricing system at about $17 per barrel. This held for ten years, with the Saudis acting as the accelerator and the brake in attempts to keep the price equitable. The Saudi royals understood that it was wiser to keep the Western world's economies on an even keel, than it was to stagger constantly from high to low and back again. Besides, America was their playground, where they could indulge their repressed fantasies out of sight of Wahhabism. Currently oil in Saudi Arabia is cheaper than bottled water.

In the interim, Saddam Hussein attacked Kuwait. The first Iraq war was occasioned by Kuwait drilling horizontally into Iraq and stealing its oil, which resulted in the attempted destruction of the Kuwaiti oil fields. The second Iraqi war (which had nothing whatsoever to do with weapons of mass destruction, but had plenty to do with oil) eventually followed, along with the subsequent destruction of Iraq and the rise of Sunni fundamentalism.

During all this, oil prices were kept within reasonable bounds by the saving grace of Saudi Arabia. Having once thought Iraq was poised to invade the kingdom, it was mightily pleased to have the US put paid to that possibility. And gas and oil prices remained stable, month after month, year after year, as James Kunstler points out,

> "With gas remaining cheap, employment rising and the computer revolution promising a new economy, the American public entered a decade-long sleepwalk of complacency. The only troubles being the disappointing slide in stock valuations and the extraordinary melt-down of Internet based dot-com businesses that were supposed to form the infra structure of the New Economy."

Then one beautiful September morning, in the eastern United States, nineteen Islamic maniacs, fifteen of them Saudi Arabians, hijacked four airliners and changed everything.

Oil is not just an energy source for heating your home, running your car and all the trucks, trains, planes, cargo boats, cruise ships, and combine harvesters in the world. It's a critical lubricant that greases every single piece of moving machinery on the planet. When it's gone and there's nothing truly viable to replace it, make no mistake: we are gone – millions of us.

You are a damn lucky adult. Do you know that? You have been (and are still) living in the most luxurious part of the tail end of the Industrial Revolution, which officially started in Britain in 1760, and so far, is still going strong. God, fate, circumstance, serendipity, the whim of the universe, whatever it was, dropped you into this planet's history flawlessly. This period of plenty, based exclusively on oil and gas, will never come again. **Never!**

Since the Second World War you have driven cars, vans, camperhomes, and trucks without a thought. Since the late Forties and Fifties, you have enjoyed central heating, put the lights on whenever needed, and flown to Spain or Portugal on holiday. Now you are enjoying double-glazing, laptop computers, smart phones, 3D televisions, laminated flooring, polyester, nylon and acrylics – all made from derivatives of oil.

If you are thirty-five or older, you arrived on this circular spaceship spinning its way through space-time at precisely the right historical moment. Much earlier, unless you were extremely rich or extremely lucky, you would have found life hard. If you didn't end up in jail as a suffragette or find yourself nursing the wounded in the Great War, or die going 'over the top' into relentless machine gun fire, you might have expired or been rendered crippled or homeless (or both) from a V2 rocket in the Second World War. If you are American you may have died as one of 100,000 troops who attacked Iwo Jima in 1945 or be lying face-down on a beach in Normandy.

Either way, you would have laboured long hours for pitiful wages, grappled with coal fires and tin baths (in the UK that is), and walked or cycled almost everywhere. If you go back just a little further, your children climbed chimneys and pulled coal wagons on their hands and knees, while you struggled to simply survive.

Go further back still, and the pre-industrial, pre-steam, pre-oil planet was not a paradise for ordinary people. It was difficult to get from point A to point B unless you owned a horse, and foreign travel was reserved for the very rich (or immigrants to the New World in a leaky wooden sailing ship).

Everything was local. You went to school locally, you shopped locally, you worked locally (probably in agriculture) and you were buried locally, all accompanied by a strong possibility that you had never travelled to Belfast or Edinburgh or Manchester or Birmingham or Cardiff or London, or any large town in your vicinity in your entire life. Horizons were limited to about a twenty-mile radius. Life was short, hard, and sometimes quite brutal.

Then came the steam age and there were some minor improvements, at least in the available radius. But the big improvements did not arrive until the oil arrived in quantity – and even then, not until it was possible to gaze around and tick off the products made from derivatives of oil – and the realisation that there are hundreds of thousands of them.

Since the discovery of the first oilfield in Pennsylvania in 1859 we have all gradually become entirely dependent on the released energy of algae, plankton, kerogen, dead dinosaurs and marine animals, to an extent that is beyond belief, beyond politics, beyond initial expectations, and now–*almost beyond recovery*.

Currently Venezuela has the largest remaining reserves, amounting to 300,878 billion barrels, followed by Saudi Arabia with some 266,455 billion barrels. It gradually diminishes country by country, mostly throughout the Middle East and with smaller fields all across Europe, from Albania to Scotland and the North Sea, with an available world total of approximately 1,726.685 billion barrels. But this includes *probable* reserves and *possible* reserves.

'Probable reserves' are those estimated to be commercially recoverable with a 50 percent possibility. 'Possible reserves' are the most speculative; they are estimated to exist and be commercially recoverable, but with only a probability of 10 percent.

That's still a heck of a lot, is it not? One heck of a lot! But it's still finite. Water is not finite because it rains. It circulates. What comes down goes back up. But oil does not. It does not rain oil, and we are using it up at 96 million barrels per day. Venezuela's millions of migrants and extreme poverty show all to clearly what can happen when the oil wells become uneconomic, or finally run out.

Kazakhstan, which has one of the last of the truly immense fields on the planet still full of oil, has some 30 billion barrels of oil in reserve. That also sounds like a lot, does it not? But in fact if all the other fields ran dry it could, in theory, supply the world for less than a year.

It could be – and it is – consistently argued that electric cars or hydrogen fuel cell cars, allied to the new Manchester technology of drawing hydrogen from the atmosphere (see below), will make sufficient difference for the oil to last a hundred years when, by which time, it simply won't be needed. However, for that circumstance to even come close, we are going to need hydrogen fuel cell tractors, trucks, and trains, plus hydrogen fuel cell cruise ships and planes. Oh! And of course, hydrogen fuel celled politicians to make some eclectic and electric decisions ... but it's not going to happen.

At least, it's not going to happen in time. Even though Japan will showcase 100 hydrogen buses at the 2020 Tokyo Olympics, along with the South Koreans who say they intend to be running 1000 hydrogen buses by 2022. London also hopes to get in on the act by trialling some London taxis and police cars within the next ten years. Unfortunately, by 2040 the world is estimated to contain two billion cars and well over nine billion people, by which time the oil (hence the petrol) will be almost gone and the price more than ten times the current price.

In 2015 Mark Jacobson, of Stanford University in California, published a strongly worded blueprint paper on how America *must* shift its economy exclusively to renewables such as wind, solar, and hydro by 2050, not just for electricity but for *all* its energy needs. Jacobson, et al., calculated a twenty-five-fold increase was necessary within thirty-five years. This award-winning roadmap was then extended to 139 countries that currently accounted for 99 percent of global emissions.

The problem of course is that 100 percent renewable energy sources, namely wind, sun, and even hydro, are dependent on the weather. The sun sinks and sometimes doesn't shine at all. The wind drops and the seasons vary. The supply can therefore plummet just when local demand is peaking.

Even if an unexpected breakthrough occurred – a stroke of pure genius, a means of ensuring future energy needs are going to be catered to – because of the availability of cheap oil and gas, such a breakthrough will struggle for funds and recognition, outside of universities such as Stanford and specialist laboratories.

Nevertheless, that breakthrough, that stroke of genius, may have just happened.

Two major problems have hampered and will continue to hamper the prospect of fuel cells powering cars, trucks and planes. The first is the cost of isolating hydrogen from anything other than natural gas or coal (which creates huge amounts of CO_2); the second is building an infrastructure to deliver that hydrogen to the aforesaid cars, trucks, tanks, and planes. The twenty-one centimetre signal of hydrogen, might show it to be the most prevalent gas in the universe, but it is still hard to come by. Its molecules are so light that the newly formed earth lost almost all of it into space. Nevertheless, Dr Moritz Kuehnel, of Swansea University, a university close to where I live, has found a way to make hydrogen out of waste plastic: any type of waste plastic. It doesn't even have to be cleaned. The process involves adding a light-absorbing material, placing it all in a solution, and exposing it to sunlight. This is really good news and may be an efficient way of getting rid of unwanted plastic. Don't forget, all plastic is a by-product of fossil fuel, so we are simply turning full circle – but it's a start.

Professor Sir Andre Geim – a Nobel laureate and winner of the Niels Bohr Medal – and his team at the University of Manchester have recently made another huge breakthrough that will affect the hydrogen economy enormously. They have shown that a two-dimensional, one-atom-thick material known as graphene and hexagonal boron nitride (h-BN), which was previously thought to be entirely impermeable, will actually allow protons to pass through.

The impact of this discovery is that it will become significantly easier to isolate hydrogen, and it will *not* be necessary to build a country-wide infrastructure for delivering hydrogen to vehicles. The fuel cells, in combination with some external energy source, will be able to produce their own hydrogen from the moist surrounding air.

It was a surprise discovery, made during research that was later peer reviewed and published in the prestigious British journal *Nature.* There it was noted that monolayer's (single layers) of graphene, combined with h-BN, are permeable to thermal protons under ambient conditions. This means that if you strip hydrogen atoms of their single electron, the isolated proton can now slip right through the two-dimensional matrix.

I can hear you now. So what! You are saying. What's that to me?

I must admit, it doesn't sound like much does it? But oh boy! It means you will, eventually, after a lot more research and development, be able to extract hydrogen from the air around you and drive your car on it. Free energy!

Free energy ... That will cause some gnashing of teeth, as well as the possibility of the invention being seized before it has even seen the light of day. After all, the American inventor Stan Meyer had a car running on water years ago. The entire concept was seized by the National Security Agency and forcibly shut down.

In 1998 Stan Meyer ran from a restaurant screaming that he had been poisoned. He later died, surrounded by the (misplaced) popular scuttlebutt that the device did not work because Meyer had deliberately not published or patented the final ingredients needed. Nevertheless, his drawings sold for a vast sum, and the purchasing company that finally managed, after much effort, to make the water fuel cell work again, was warned off once more by a National Security Order. The purchasers are currently looking for a country, other than the USA, to produce the product (see Dr Steven Greer lecture, re: Stan Meyer).

Originally it was thought that single-layer graphene was so impermeable that nothing could ever penetrate. When it was finally discovered that protons could be passed through it, the shock could be felt in Birmingham. It was once thought the time involved for a hydrogen atom to pass through this material had to be on the order of 13.8 billion years, the known lifetime of the universe. That is how all fuel cells operate, by conducting protons while not allowing gasses through: the so-called polymer exchange membrane fuel cell (PEMFC).

Modern fuel cell membranes are made from polymers that quite accidentally allow fuel to pass through, which limits both their durability and efficiency. The Manchester team's efforts suggest that 2D graphene and h-BN, can now be used to create a more efficient thinner membrane, reducing fuel crossover and the subsequent cell poisoning.

The key to this whole miracle discovery: this scientific eureka moment in history is that this particular two-dimensional membrane harvests hydrogen (the most abundant element in the entire universe) out of the air as you actually drive your car along the road.

> "When you know how it should work, it's a very simple setup. You put a hydrogen containing gas on one side, apply a small electric current, and collect hydrogen on the other side. This hydrogen can then be burned in a fuel cell."

Said, Marcelo Lozada-Hidalgo, a PhD student and co-author of the paper. He then added,

> "We worked with small membranes and the achieved flow of hydrogen is of course tiny so far. But this is the initial stage of discovery, and the paper is to make experts aware of the existing prospects. To build up and test hydrogen harvesters will require much further effort."

The often-quoted example of splitting *water*, rather than air, into oxygen and hydrogen, does not apparently work in a fuel cell situation because standard physics dictates that the amount of energy required to do so exceeds the energy needed to combine them again in a fuel cell (notwithstanding the secret was discovered by Stan Meyer and suppressed a long time ago).

Rice University researchers in Maine and Houston, Texas, have also discovered that it's possible to obtain graphene-based quantum dots from coal, and that this new material actually outperforms platinum-based catalysts in fuel cell reactions. Said Professor James Tour, a Rice University chemist,

> "You don't need to apply as high a voltage as you do with

platinum to get the oxygen reduction reaction to occur. We also get about seventy percent higher current than what platinum would offer."

*

You may think – *well there we are then!* Problem solved! It is of course extremely interesting, and if the Manchester discovery lives up to its promise, and the Rice discovery makes for cheaper catalytic reactions, and everybody concerned (particularly politicians) takes the bull by the horns, and they all move at a speed consistent with promotion or taking a bribe, then *maybe, just maybe*, our children, and children's children, will not face such a bleak, cataclysmic future after all.

However, you and I know, that's extremely unlikely, and all the problems previously outlined remain. They haven't gone away because BP is experimenting with used oil and cooking fat, or because Manchester has had a breakthrough and Rice has published a revolutionary paper. Oil is cheap, gas is cheap and, according to one Oxford expert, will stay that way for a long time yet.

If that is the case, there will be very few renewables on the horizon, no matter how efficient, because politicians and business moguls will always opt for the cheaper, easier, and already understood option. Which automatically leads us to another question: even if oil prices do hold – can we afford to keep using it? Are we not simply creating a race against time: a race between sufficient renewables to exist in some measure of future comfort, and global warming? This is a race we are currently losing – but cannot possibly afford to lose.

*

Possibilities for the Western world to survive: for the UK to survive, for America to survive. For that matter, anywhere on the planet to survive, depend on the above possibilities and technologies and other types of renewable energy taking off like a

Soyuz rocket, plus the immediate building of several nuclear power stations. The power stations would at least take care of the electricity (although the spent fuel is still the most critical environmental problem) and the hydrogen fuel cells would take care of transport.

(Stephen Hawking has suggested that nuclear fusion, if developed, would solve all our problems forever. NF is the process in which two atomic nuclei are fused together into a larger single nucleus, releasing energy in the process. The technique has already been demonstrated, but needs vast sums of money and the political will to proceed further.)

Like most of the other problems we are facing, the spent fuel problem from current power stations could be resolved by shooting tankers of the stuff into the sun. The problem, as ever, is cost.

But all the above would seem to be a pipe dream. If the predictions about peak oil and gas are correct – and that's the key to all of this: that's the $64,000 question – if they are correct? Then it cannot be done in time. Not in our lifetime: certainly not in my lifetime. No way! Besides if the oil and gas are so cheap, why bother? Particularly when certain famous Oxford academics are still insisting there is enough oil in the ground to compete with the Atlantic Ocean.

Why cannot it be completed in time? Because human beings are not like that; *we* are not like that. We are slow to act in the first place, even slower to perform, and blindingly short-sighted. All political systems are short- sighted. So, we will continue using oil and gas. Currently oil is being used worldwide, at just under 100 million barrels per day, over 36 billion barrels, or 11 billion tonnes a year. A barrel contains 35 imperial gallons, 42 US gallons.

Rates of vehicle ownership in India and China are set to soar. Plus, industrialisation and electrical grid construction in large areas of China, India, Indonesia, and even Africa, will continue to drive dramatic increases in oil and gas consumption in the next decade or two. At the current rate *(only the current rate)* of consumption, it is thought that oil will run out *completely* by 2052. Thirty-four years from now. Not fifty-three, as previously predicted. Not a hundred, as spun by the Saudis. Not *never* as spun by some economists...*Thirty-four*!

(And as you have already seen, some well-known experts predict only twenty years– even ten!)

In the meantime, the current rate of consumption will increase as developing nations, who have traditionally used the minimum amounts, come on stream. They won't be left behind and they won't suddenly be driving hydrogen fuel cell cars. No matter what Manchester or Rice have discovered, they will be driving petroleum or diesel cars. And I can assure you they are not going to say, 'Good morning gentlemen how are you all today? We know of course that the oil is running out, but don't worry, we'll let that overweight clown America and that pompous John Bull and that old trollop Europe, take the balance. What the hell! We're used to slumming it.'

So, in short, multiple experts anticipate that oil will run out long before the predicted 2052 arrives, and gas by 2062 and, eventually coal (assuming certain countries continue to use it, which, if they do, will *hopefully* use full carbon capture as an essential technology). And of course, before they actually run out – in fact, well before they actually run out – the price will make using the stuff impossible. No one will be able to afford it. Except perhaps the military, who will grab the last drops whenever and wherever they can, as if dying from thirst in the Sahara.

All these energy sources were free. We had, of course, to pay to extract them from the Earth, but they were nevertheless gifts. Gifts from God if you like, gifts from nature, gifts from the planet's pre-history. But Christmas will soon be over. There will be no more free lunches. We will have to actually make, or grow, or travel somewhere else *(such as the Moon or another planet)* to mine the alternatives.

And although sugar cane oil, corn oil, palm oil, rape seed and various vegetable oils, and a host of other available oil-producing plants, will fill some of the oil energy gap, they will not produce even one quarter of the necessary amount which, by 2050 to 2060, will be absolutely gargantuan.

Incidentally, how many people know that a good percentage of the diesel you put in your car is already palm oil, which increases (not decreases) carbon emissions? Loopholes in international carbon accounting rules mean that biomass emissions are not counted as carbon emissions, but as carbon neutral. *Which they most certainly are not!* (*New Scientist,* 5 May 2018, p22.)

By 2050, within the lifetime of my kids and yours, the bubble will have burst; the party (as the oil expert Richard Heinberg says) will be over – and it won't be pretty.

To avoid this scenario, we need to act now: find out how quickly and efficiently we can use renewables such as hydrogen, biomass, and nuclear, as energy sources, keeping what oil remains, plus using every known viable alternative, including Waste To Energy (WTE).

WTE does have remarkable potential in the distant future, as does hydrogen. WTE means using food waste, animal waste, all kinds of plant waste, even human waste, and converting it to biomass. It can be done. But the technology has to be thoroughly researched and the possibility of equalling 96 million barrels a day given serious consideration.

Some people, the Saudi government included, think the oil age will end long before we actually run out of oil, because of the possibilities inherent in all the various renewable methods of obtaining energy. A Saudi minister has reportedly commented that, "The Stone Age did not run out of stone, it improved its technology and moved on."

Well, splendid. I'm all for improving technology. I think the Manchester discovery could well be a life saver – *way into the future.* The wind, the sea, the sun, plus the biomass of abandoned school dinners, along with you and your dog's poo are, in all respects, just as free as the oil in the ground. Unfortunately, sophisticated computer projections have shown, many times over, that unless huge inputs of cash – equivalent to the finances involved in attempts to get back to the Moon and the intended journey to Mars – are made available RIGHT NOW, these types of alternative energy sources are going to remain just that: alternative.

At the CERAWeek conference in Houston, the Saudi Aramco CEO, Amin Nasser, had the following to say,

> "Many people wrongly believe that it is a simple matter of electric vehicles quickly and smoothly replacing the internal combustion engine. But the path toward cutting carbon emissions is a lot more complicated than that. While it should be a global priority to improve efficiency and cut emissions from internal combustion engines and fuels, pure electric and hydrogen cars still face a range of problems."

During the week-long meeting (CERAWeek is an annual energy conference organised by IHS Markit), Nasser noted that electric cars still depend on a power grid, and in markets like China and India, emission-intensive coal still supplies half the available power. He has said,

> "Right now with battery-electric vehicles, *we are simply moving emissions from tailpipe to smokestack.* So yes; battery electric vehicles will grow and have a welcome role to play in global mobility, but given the competition and complexity of the transition their impact on the twenty percent oil demand should not be exaggerated. That still

> leaves the other eighty percent, where oil demand con-
> tinues to grow."

There is of course another problem not mentioned by Amin Nasser, because he doesn't want to rock the boat sufficient for it to founder.

Many families in the so-called developed world own two, three, or even four cars (possibly including a camper). How do you charge all these cars on a single-phase 240/50 volt circuit at the same time or even on the same day? It's been suggested by a politician (*not*, I might add, the previous female politicians) that a new multiple charging system will be attached to every lamp post.

Ha! ... Typical politician... He obviously knows zilch about electricity. To carry such loads as well as service all the houses plus the street lights at tea time (or any time), it would have to be, at the very least, a 3phase set up running beneath the street or pavement, with a step-down transformer fitted within every lamppost (or somewhere else convenient) causing truly mas-sive infrastructure renewal and huge national expense. In add-ition, it would have to be installed along every street, in every town in the country.

Do you think, the said politician, had given a single thought to what kind of local generating stations are going to run this extra load? Not the current ones, that's for sure. Plus all the houses in the UK (including Europe), are supposed to be heated by electri-city within fifteen years.

Numerous nuclear power stations (like in France) might be the answer. But where are they? You don't have to be some kind of expert. You just need to look around you. It's an impossible scenario!

We also all know of course that neither the wind, nor the sea, nor the sun, can propel a combine harvester, a school bus, an ocean liner, or an aeroplane (but the energy available from biomass or hydrogen, might, if applied in time). Neither can the wind or the sun be used to make various plastics and other necessary products, such as our footballs, our phones, our light switches and sockets, our computers, our TVs, our food wrappings, our double-glazed window frames, our clothes, our carpets and flooring, our fishing nets, our fertilisers, our car tyres, our perfumes and pharmaceuticals, our asphalt for the roads, our this and that...oh heck! The list is endless and they are all made from derivatives of oil. And of course we are all aware that plastics are polluting the food chain via the fish in the oceans, to a degree that an expert such as Abigail Entwistle, at Conservation Science and Design, calls it a veritable time-bomb.

No matter what Professor Dieter Helm, a well-known and respected Oxford economist has to say – *and he says it a lot* – oil prices will eventually go up. In fact, as supply begins to diminish, the price of oil will go absolutely through the roof: even a £100 a gallon is entirely possible. And unless viable alternatives are found, car journeys, plane journeys, ferry and ship journeys, will, of course cease. Food will climb to staggering prices and become virtually unobtainable, as trucks and trains will have to pay insane prices for fuel. And even if by then, they are partly electric, or even fully hydrogen driven (which is extremely unlikely) they will still need lubrication.

We are facing several major world problems of enormous catastrophic consequence, but at least two are imminent (aside from Bush's, Cheney's and Blair's initial contributions to Islamic mayhem, followed by Putin and Saudi Arabia). I won't see them, and maybe you won't see them, because we both fell into the history of the Industrial Revolution serendipitously. But my kids, your kids, and especially their kids, will most definitely see them – and we are doing very little about it.

There are some considerations given to the thought that the fossil fuel problem will solve the global warming problem, in that, as the oil runs out, it will stop atmospheric CO_2 emissions.

Well, in a sense that's true. Clearly, if we have no more fossil fuels to burn, there will be limited CO_2 emissions. But will it happen in time? At the present speed – no it will not!

Atmospheric greenhouse gasses are at their highest levels in human history and, in fact, at their highest for over 800,000 years. The ten hottest years on record have occurred since 1997. Currently (January 2018), Florida has deep snow for the first time since 1939 and huge storms are sweeping across the Atlantic, blasting the Caribbean and tail ending in Europe. Floods are occurring everywhere it normally rains, while elsewhere fires dominate the landscape, such as in Greece and California. The Mendocino Complex fire in California scorched more than 120,000 hectares of land and occupied the efforts of over 14,000 fire-fighters.

Paradise, in Bute County, California, a town of over 26,000 people is no longer a paradise. It's been burnt to the ground, and over seventy-one people killed and almost a thousand missing. These fires will continue to cause catastrophic damage as well as loss of life. And this is just the beginning.

In Nawabshah, Pakistan, the highest April temperature ever recorded on Earth occurred in 2018. The Pakistan Meteorological Department recorded the highest temperature at 50.2C. For two months running the region set a new temperature record with the heat soaring to a national record of 45.5C (113.9F). The local newspaper *Dawn* reported dozens had fainted after suffering heatstroke and described the weather as 'unbearable'. The UK recorded its hottest day in April since 1949, with temperatures in London reaching 29.1C (84.4F).

Nine out of ten climate scientists, recently polled, thought that a two-degree rise in global temperatures will soon be exceeded. Such a rise could result in 20 to 30 percent of species facing extinction.

The Met Office has warned that, in order to prevent the most severe effects of climate change, we need to curb emissions of CO_2 and other harmful gasses to levels well below those of today. Electricity generation from conventional fossil fuel sources is responsible for over 30 percent of the UK's carbon emissions, making it the single largest contributor.

In America the situation is far worse and plainly ludicrous. The current establishment, which appears to have serious mental problems, refuses to recognise the facts of global warming and the bizarre weather it produces, and considers it fake news, even while Florida is covered in snow and California burns to a crisp.

Clearly one problem precedes the other. Global warming is a phenomenon that cannot much longer be ignored. We might be able to head-in-the-sand, the possibility of running out of oil in twenty to thirty odd years – *at least for now* – but we cannot ignore the warming of the atmosphere because that problem is imminent and the solutions accelerating away from us ever faster. It's even been suggested that climate models are insufficiently robust and that true climate sensitivity could be six degrees centigrade or more (*New Scientist*, 27 January 2018, p23).

In America, the only really intelligent individual appears to be Al Gore, a sort of Lone Ranger of common sense, amidst a rafter of turkeys. Believe it or not, American policy makers are currently talking about restoring the coal age. Trump has taken a lot of slack for that (no pun intended), but the administration is turning an entirely deaf ear to the world's climate experts.

The Attorney General of the State of New York has recently launched an investigation into ExxonMobil for fraud, in its various attempts to deliberately funnel money into the denial that global warming is real. So real in fact, that we are currently putting 110 billion tons of fossil fuel gasses into the atmosphere: EVERY SINGLE DAY. Effectively we are using the thin layer of atmosphere surrounding our planet like a running sewer.

> "When you're born you get a ticket to the freak show. If you're born in America you get a front row seat."

Famously said by the American stand-up George Carlin. He should have added, 'Especially when the Republicans cannot control their pet gargoyle.'

*

Hydrogen *can* be obtained from coal by reacting coal with oxygen and steam under high pressure and temperature to form a synthesis gas consisting of hydrogen and carbon monoxide. However, its manufacture is a filthy process that puts more pollution into the atmosphere than even conventional fossil fuels.

This method of obtaining hydrogen is possible, but is considered by climatologists a non- starter. There are much better ways to obtain hydrogen; but because of the backward stance of the Republicans in America, they may not be on the cards for some years to come. Coal can also be used conventionally for many things, as long as *full carbon capture takes place*, and the carbon is buried deep underground. Unfortunately, this is all too often not the case.

In an attempt to 'make it the case', twenty-one young people, some of them children, are taking the US government to court. Nine-year-old Levi is quoted by the *New Scientist* journal as saying, "It's scary, having someone in the White House who doesn't believe in climate change."

The plaintiffs are accusing the government of decades of deceit and wrong-headedness in handling climate change. Currently there are eleven hundred outstanding lawsuits worldwide invoking climate change. The principal behind the lawsuits is that something must be done to counter the effects of global warming. One of those principles (in fact a major part of the argument) is that CO_2 could be captured from power station chimneys and exhausts and stored underground, but little attention and even less financing has been directed to this end throughout the world.

And not at all in America!

There has already been some success in this area of endeavour. In 2015 the Dutch environmental group Urgenda won the first-citizen-led litigation case against a government. Its legal team successfully argued that Holland was not doing enough to avert climate change. The court ordered the government to reduce CO_2 emissions throughout the Nederland's by 25 percent by 2020. This is clearly an area of protest we should all be looking at, because it's doable.

Gus Speth, a previous senior advisor to President Jimmy Carter in the 1970s, has publicly stated that,

> "The federal government knowingly set and stayed a course for major climate change, with terrible consequences to be endured especially by present-day young people and future generations. It is the greatest dereliction of civic responsibility in the history of the republic."

With regard to the above, the New York investment bank, Jefferies, has intimated that coal is not going to decline at all: not in the slightest. It has raised its target price of seaborne thermal coal, burned to make steam for electricity generation, as opposed to coking coal used for making steel and iron, from £68 to £80 per ton for the remainder of 2018, with a long- term lift of from £49 to £63 per ton. This is because third world countries, intent on competing at any price in the world market, have no current alternative but to burn coal. Which of course is absolutely disastrous for global warming without full carbon capture – a process which I guarantee will not happen!

A recent uninformed article (not their usual practise) in *New Scientist* assumed there is optimism with reference to global warming. This article followed the same head-in-the-sand view inherent in all governments with reference to the issue of oil depletion. As if simply being buoyant, even flippant, about global warming (or oil depletion) will somehow solve these problems – or that talking equally glibly about biomass and hydrogen cells will magic the required results. It won't!

Here is a reproduced letter to *New Scientist* 6 January 2018, by a gentleman called Marc Smith-Evans, who lives in Bagabag, Nueva Vizcaya, in the Philippines. I'm sure he won't mind. He is, after all a retired expert telling the truth as he sees it: and although no expert, that's what I am trying to do

> *Your recent leader suggests that we should be optimistic about the future of the biosphere (New Scientist 9 December, 2017. p5). I don't share this optimism. When I graduated in the late 1960s nobody was an 'environmentalist' – the concept didn't exist then. However my career led me down a path that identified me as an environmental scientist. In this role I have worked in many countries, for client, consultant and contractor, to champion the environmental cause. Sadly the overall impact that I have had has been pitiful, a sentiment shared by my peers. We haven't been effective, despite a strong desire to protect our planet. Simply put, the power brokers, developers, politicians and investors have done little more than pay lip service to the environmental cause: the adage that every victory is temporary, and every defeat permanent, summarises the view of those who care about our planet. In more than forty years I have seen many defeats and very few victories. The health of the biosphere isn't going to get better, only the rate of deterioration can be ameliorated by those who care, and there are precious few of us with any power to affect change. Where are the leaders who advocate **a better environment for our children?*** (My emphasis)

A good question – and it's a planet-wide issue. It's as obvious as a boil on your face and cannot simply be ignored. In the meantime, the problem is seriously exacerbated by fruitcakes like Donald Trump, et al., who theoretically represent the most powerful people on the planet. He (or they) may have stopped believing in liberal democracy by instigating the latecomers' need for coal, but I very much doubt they realise what the implications are. The trouble with Trump is he never engages his brain (assuming its findable) before he opens a tweet. He has managed to morph the oft repeated statement, 'Make America Great Again' into 'Make America Hate Again.'

Bringing the American presidency into international disrepute by running a sort of personal Barnum and Bailey show, in which everyone gets fired, and featuring the porn star Stormy Daniels, is one thing. Accusing Obama of using the FBI to tap his phone (which Comey, the FBI director, denied had happened, and anyway couldn't happen), plus ignoring the 'Government Ethics Program' to the point where its director, Walter Michael Shaub, felt obliged to resign in July 2017, because, as he said, "There are no ethics to be found in this presidency," is entirely another. And the reasons are not hard to find. Trump has used every single opportunity to publicise his businesses by using Trump Tower (which incidentally he doesn't own) for official government occasions and by promoting his other businesses in his usual childishly boastful manner.

He further uses the presidency of the United States as a monetising piggy bank, ingratiatingly associating himself with the hopelessly corrupt leaders of corrupt countries, such as llham Aliyev of Azerbaijan, Crown Prince Mohammad bin Salman of Saudi Arabia and Vladimir Putin of the Russian Federation.

And of course, if you have no standards, no real ethical or moral stricture, a very short attention span and merely a pretence of interest in Christianity in order to influence the southern Christian right, you are not going to give a toss about global warming, or the fossil fuel problem, or even the insane butchery of a Turkish journalist. You are only ever going to be concerned with how much money and showbiz-like prestige it's possible to get out of this presidency malarkey.

Worse than any of the above, Ricken Patel-Avaaz, the Oxford graduate president of Avaaz, a major global online activist organisation with 43 million subscribers, has categorically stated that Trump has not been able to finance himself via American banks since the 1990s, because of his incessant bankruptcies. Instead, he is using, and has used, oligarch money laundered in Russia via criminal activity to finance his various schemes in the US and elsewhere, such as Scotland. And that he is well aware of how this money is obtained. (*After the fall of communism the KGB and every other Russian government agency looted Russia of its wealth, and with the complicity of the West, placed the looted money in banks in London and New York. The scale of looting was unprecedented, in the history of the world, and helped to cause the moral decline of the West to this very day.*)

As well as being complicit in this activity Felix Sater, Trump's adviser and financial broker, is a Russian born convicted felon, who wrote the following email to Trump's lawyer Michael Cohen, in November 2015, as reprinted in *The New York Times*, 27 August, 2017:

> *Michael I arranged for Ivanka to sit in Putin's private chair at his desk and in his office in the Kremlin. I will get Putin on this program and we will get Donald elected. We both know no one else knows how to pull this off without stupidity or greed getting in the way. I know how to play it and we can get this done. Buddy our boy can become President of the USA and we can engineer it. I will get all of Putin's team to buy in on this. I will.*

Effectively Russia (along with the religious loonies of the right) has managed, via stealth and due diligence, to place a corrupt individual of their creation in the White House. We have to ignore him and his views in the hope he will not survive: and he may not survive for a second term.

Even if a sensible Social Democrat like Bernie Saunders manages to fund himself onto centre stage, the toxic and immoral scourge that is Trump "et al"., will have poisoned the American taste buds for decades.

Whatever the outcome we cannot waste a minute: not a minute! We need to start worrying now, and to find serious alternatives to fossil fuels before fossil fuels expire, for *two* reasons.

One; is because if we run with oil and gas to the end – the end of millions will quickly follow. Two; is because if we don't find alternatives soon, we will cook in our streets like burgers on a griddle, and all the animals will die, including cows and sheep and horses, and even elephants and kangaroos. And in Europe, which traditionally has little in the way of air-conditioning (even if they could afford the fuel to run it) people will expire by the hundreds of thousands, holding hands on their own beds in their own homes.

*

Global problems, natural or manmade, cause the frontal lobes of certain unbalanced individuals to overheat and make them even more unbalanced. So, wars of attrition will be even more commonplace, and oil wars are an absolute certainty. The way to obtain the stuff you require, as far as countries are concerned, is to trade for it, politically manoeuvre for it, or fight for it. America and the UK have used all three methods to obtain precious metals (let alone oil) with political intrigue, deliberate local interference, and consummate bribery on a grand scale, in order to promote national instability, which they have used and still use in places like the Congo and the Middle East.

The Democratic (except it isn't at all democratic) Republic of Congo (DRC) supplies over 70 percent of the world's supply of tantalum, an ingredient in all mobile phones and nuclear reactors. It also supplies columbite-tantalite, coltan, cassiterite and wolframite. Coltan is the ore from which tantalum is extracted, while cassiterite ore produces tin. There are gold, diamonds and vast amounts of copper. In the east of the country oil and gas are mined; it contains the second largest deposit of crude oil in Africa (Angola having the first) and currently 25,000 barrels a day are exported.

Now go take a look at the plight of that country, assuming you can find a decent road or railway to travel down. The DRC, it is said by academia, has patently failed to reap significant benefits from its huge natural resources (a polite way of putting it), and currently ranks 186 out of 187 countries on the United Nations human development index. So, who has actually benefitted? Who do you think?

The ground in the Congo is a veritable cash-cow it produces billions of dollars or pound sterling or whatever currency you prefer. What it doesn't produce is integrity, honesty, concern for the plight of the workers or the population at large who live mostly in abject poverty. The sight of their plight caused by deliberate destabilisation and conflict is disgusting, revolting and outrageous. But who cares? Certainly not the same people *unconcerned* about the future loss of oil and global warming – the very people who control our lives.

How many people does it occur to that politicians – all politicians – from presidents to local councillors are just bog-standard people? They are not experts. They are not specialists. Although there are degrees in politics in general, there are no degrees to *become* a politician: all you have to be is determined and pushy. The more you can act nice one minute and be a real shit the next, the more chance for success.

And, of course, it is these people who tell us what to do, who make laws and decisions that affect all our lives. Why, for example, isn't the Minister for Universities and Science, a scientist? Because he most certainly is not! In fact, he is currently Boris Johnson's younger brother, who studied modern history at Oxford.

Why wasn't the Secretary of State for Education an ex-school inspector, or a headmaster, or headmistress, because again, she most certainly was not? She was, until January 2018, when she resigned from the government, the attractive Justin Greening, who has an MBA in business studies, but what the hell did she know about national, grand scale education and how to improve it (because it definably needs improving)? Not a lot, I suggest. And in my opinion, neither does her replacement, the Robin Williams look-alike, Damien Hinds, who read philosophy at Oxford. Meanwhile, she is screaming hard about Brexit, with about as much inside information as my local postman.

None of them are sufficiently qualified. And in America we have the grand vision of a notorious Tweeting fruitcake with a child's attention span, a debatable intelligence quotient, and an apparent desire to terminate North Korea with extreme violence or to curry favour with its murderously autocratic leader, Kim Jong-Un.

Such a union, although definitely not made in heaven, might *just* defuse the North/South Korean situation in the long term, or they might defuse the tension themselves outside of any American involvement. We shall see? It is these same people, these same governments everywhere that keep saying,

'No problem folks: take it easy! We will solve the oil problem and the over-heating problem and the rising sea problem, along with the over-population problem and the coming unstoppable health and diseases problem, and the drug problem, and the water problem, and the consequent food problems which will surely follow the oil shortages, etc., etc., because we are politicians, we are experts – *we know what we are doing.*'

Yeah! Sure...

The military will require huge volumes of oil in storage in order to fight for the remaining oil. And they *will* fight for it. An aircraft carrier such as the USS Nimitz, for example, although propelled by a nuclear reactor, also carries three million gallons of aviation fuel, so you can imagine the storage needed as the oil disappears and frantic efforts are made to control the last of the available fields. And we are talking thirty-four years (or considerably less) from now.

When the hammer starts to fall most countries (unlike the United States, which has vast stores of oil in caverns), including Great Britain, have little more than a few days' reserve, and will therefore be in serious trouble. This is notwithstanding that the policies of the European Union have reduced the British farming industry to a country pub joke. Within weeks we will be unable to feed our own people from our own resources, because there will be precious little of those resources, and currently thousands of agricultural fields are lying entirely empty.

Just take a walk or a drive (while you can) through the countryside. Pleasant as it undoubtedly is, note how empty of crops it is. We are in 2018 and are already in the cow dung (but not the biofuel). Because if, in future, ships cannot deliver food as a result of the expense, then the fact that they have not been converted to run on liquid hydrogen, hydrogen fuel cells, or biofuel energy, means that we starve. (Many cargo ships use bunker fuel: thick sludgy oil that emits 3,500 times more sulphur dioxide than diesel. The product is banned in several coastal routes, including the English Channel).

*

The popular opinion in America, and elsewhere, is that the US invaded Iraq because their intelligence was considered correct, and that Saddam Hussein had reneged on his promise and was continuing with his nuclear and chemical weapons ambitions. Therefore, the country posed a severe threat because it harboured weapons of mass destruction (WMD).

But in fact, it was neither the incorrect intelligence, nor the possibility of WMD. The war was the direct result of a nonsensical ideological concept held by the neoconservatives in the Republican Party that all dictatorships were a threat to democracy and they should be brought to the high table of democratic liberty – by hook or by crook (mostly crook) – and that by doing so the countries' oil reserves could somehow be transferable.

But they couldn't say that. They had to have a popular believable excuse. That excuse went catastrophically wrong and caused the biggest political cock-up since the Bay of Pigs invasion. But it was, and still is, *far worse*, since it caused an upsurge of religious fervour that balked attempts to control the oil and has so far killed over half a million people.

Former US Secretary of Defence and former Republican Senator, Chuck Hagel, has said of the war in Iraq,

> "People say we're not fighting for oil. Of course we are. They talk about America's national interest. What the hell do you think they're talking about? We're not there for figs."

General John Abizaid, the four-star former commander of CENTCOM (Central Command) with responsibility for Iraq has said that,

> "Of course it's about oil, it's very much about oil, and we can't really deny that. I am saddened that it is politically inconvenient to acknowledge what everyone knows. The Iraq war is largely about oil."

George W. Bush commented that,

> "Keeping Iraqi oil away from the bad guys was a key motive for the Iraq war. If Zarqawi and bin Laden gain control of Iraq, they would create a new training ground for future terrorist attacks. *They would seize oil fields to fund their ambitions.*"

I feel sure Ricky Gervais would see that one as heaven sent!

The reasons for the US invasion clearly had nothing whatsoever to do with weapons of mass destruction (interpreted by many cynics as 'Weapons of Mass Deception'). They knew full well that Iraq had no such weapons and the attempts to control the oil engendered a catastrophe, led by the United States and aided by the British lapdog war criminal Blair. This is what directly caused the rise of (AQ) Al-Qaeda, (AS) Al-Shabbab, (ISIL) Islamic-State-of-Iraq-and-the-Levant, (ISI) Islamic-State-of-Iraq, (AAI) Ansar-al-Islam, (ANA) Al-Nagsha-bandlya-Army, (LET) Lashkar-e-Taiba, (AAAH) Asaib-Ahl-al-Haqq, (AHAMB) Abu-Hafs-al-Masri-Brigade, (HTAS) Hayat-Tahrir-Al-Sham, formally known as Al-Nusra, including the re-emergence of the infamous Mahdi Army, and at least eight to ten other Jihadist groups who have stalked Iran, Iraq, Afghanistan, Syria, Somalia, Yemen, India, and the rest of the world ever since.

America's high-flown ideological purpose conveniently forgot to add Saudi Arabia to that list. The US and the UK appear to be perfectly happy to indulge the Saudi situation, in which 25 percent of Saudi Arabia's GDP is directed towards the support of the royal family, and where a recent secret poll showed that 50 percent of the population agreed with the generalised ideologies of Osama Bin Laden and cannot abide the Saudi royal family. Richard Heinberg, author of the oil depletion book, *The Party's Over,* has made it clear that,

> "If not for oil, the US would have little interest in the Middle East (specifically Saudi Arabia). Osama bin Laden would never have felt compelled to destroy symbols of American economic and military power...Moreover, it appeared that pre-9/11 investigations by the FBI into Al Qaeda (Al Nusra) had been systematically obstructed by orders from the highest levels of the US government, perhaps to divert attention away from certain members of the Saudi royal family and the bin Laden family, who had for years been financially supporting Osama bin Laden."

Saudi Arabia is, without question, one of the most tyrannical countries in the world, outside of North Korea. The principal form of Islam in Saudi Arabia is called Wahhabism, a very austere and repressive doctrine. No freedom of expression is allowed along with an intense repression of women's rights (effectively they have none). Yet the US and the UK, who claim to be absolutely horrified by the discrimination towards women in Islamic Syria, Iraq, Afghanistan, and virtually all the Middle East, are quite accepting of the despotic Saudi rulers. And, as we all know, justice in Saudi Arabia is little short of biblical, with limbs being amputated, public flogging of girls who have been raped, and even public beheadings as the norm.

In fact, before the recent changes in the law concerning female drivers, occasioned by the efforts of female activists, not by the prince, a nineteen-year-old female victim of a gang rape was given 200 lashes and six months imprisonment. She was dragged from her car and she and her female companion were brutally raped by seven men, who were given minor custodial sentences.

She was handed this appalling sentence because she was not, at the time, driving while accompanied by a male guardian (women must have a male counterpart when travelling anywhere; they need special permission from the family males to even go to school, to work, or open a bank account). Her male lawyer was arrested and her initial sentence of ninety-five lashes increased to 200 simply because she attempted to use the new driving law and take the matter to court (*the law about women drivers has been accompanied by a crackdown on dissenters, involving the arrests of dozens of clerics, women's rights activists and intellectuals*). That's exactly what happened in Nazi Germany.

Even more recently (October 2018) the Saudi journalist, Jamal Khashoggi, who traditionally was mildly critical of the Saudi royals, visited the Saudi Embassy in Turkey for a divorce certificate and never reappeared. The Turkish investigators discovered he had been tortured to death, and then unbelievably dismembered, apparently while still alive, and finally partly dissolved in acid and thrown down a well at the Saudi consul's home a mile from the consulate. It seems the rest of the embassy could clearly hear his screams. But will the world line up to also scream: "I hope you and the prince of evil rot in hell!" and then do something positive about it? Will anyone be arrested and summoned to the International Criminal Court? Or will the Crown Prince (who according to the CIA is complicit in the crime) choose the perpetrators he himself instigated and silence all of them instead?

Why do we do next to nothing about such unjust corrupt regimes, such as Saudi Arabia's? Could it possibly have anything to do with Saudi Arabia's Aramco that controls just about the largest oil fields in history – and the fact that Saudis traditionally came to the West's rescue when oil was needed quickly and at the right price? Surely not! Surely the West cannot be that two-faced and has more integrity than that?

Unfortunately, democracy has nothing to do with altruism and high-flown political ideology (although that's the theory). It's categorically about political and financial preservation. In the past this has included persuading (meaning gifted with planes and tanks) countries like Saudi Arabia to lower their oil prices to western countries, so as to bankrupt the old Soviet Union which, in 1991 it successfully accomplished. Afterwards the oil prices shot back up to ensure the continuing success of America's oil fields.

It isn't rocket science! It's all about power, money, and control. And that means oil. But you may be surprised to learn that Saudi Arabia is not alone in its medieval attitude towards women. Putin has passed a law that decriminalises most types of domestic violence in Russia, a country which was already awash in domestic violence. Ten thousand women a year are killed by their partners every year in Russia, and it is estimated that 36,000 a year are regularly beaten and abused. Effectively there is no longer any law in Russia that protects women from men. Over ten million women who have been forced to leave their partners because of abuse are living in extreme poverty.

Russia has also stopped funding organisations that protect women, such as safe houses or sheltered housing; women are therefore obliged to stay with their abusive, drunken partners until they are killed by them. There are five million alcoholics in Russia and nine million drug addicts. A third of all deaths are alcohol related. Russia also has the fastest growing AIDS epidemic in the world, with one and a half million known victims and possibly millions unknown, because the government entirely ignores the problem.

The facts are, according to the United Nations, that more 600 million women live in countries where sexual violence is not a crime. In the United States 15 percent of women state they have been raped in their lifetimes; in the United Kingdom 30 percent of women state they have been, at sometime, sexually abused. Worldwide, 30 percent have experienced sexual violence in their relationships, amounting to 65 percent in central sub-Saharan Africa and 16 percent in East Asia.

Again, according to the United Nations, such violence is not more prevalent where men outnumber women. Neither is it due to the reasons that certain societies are overall more liberal (such as, for example, Western Europe, Australasia and the US). Out of 156 tribal societies, 18 percent were classified as rape prone. The shared attitudes were high levels of violence in general, lack of father parenting, low respect for women, and excluding women from public, economic and political life, (as for example, in Saudi Arabia).

Russia under Putin has become far more orthodox and childishly macho, reverting to attitudes of mind that belonged, even when they were initially prevalent, to the Stone Age. The truth is that much of the history of Russia is one of extraordinary music and literature mixed with violent oppression. The classical age of beautiful cities like St Petersburg, and of writers like Pushkin, Gogol or Dostoevsky, or composers such as Tchaikovsky or Stravinsky, is long gone into the distant past. It has nothing whatsoever to do with swaggering ex-communist thugs like Putin. A previous Russian oil millionaire, Mikhail Khodokovsk, who now lives in Switzerland, has called Putin, "An envious, scheming, and greedy man."

He is of course not alone in this quest for money and fame via politics at any cost. Tony Blair has become the wealthiest ex-prime ministers of all time. During his term in office, he was as equally surrounded by sycophants as is Trump, and is now receiving thousands of pounds an hour for lectures that a first-year political student could give. Including huge sums, literally into the multi-millions of pounds, for advising extremist individuals such as Nursultan Nazarbayev, the murdering dictator of Kazakhstan, on how he might avoid western media criticism after orders to the police to shoot to kill dissatisfied oil workers and at least sixty striking miners.

To this day, no one dares question Nazarnayev's leadership. Yet Blair's Mayfair consultancy organisation is happy to act as a 'spin doctor' advising this murderous dictator, and others, such as Egypt's Abdul-Fattah al-Sisi, how they can best avoid negative publicity. The solipsistic Blair has without doubt the most impressive grasp on insincerity I have ever seen.

*

Most people – just about everybody in fact – believe that the war in Iraq and Afghanistan was instigated by three commercial aircraft flying into and destroying the Twin Towers of the World Trade Centre and the Pentagon, killing just under 3,000 people in total.

However, two French intelligence analysts, Jean-Charles Brisard and Guillaume Dasquie, disagree. They claim that President Bush, et al., halted an ongoing investigation by the CIA into the bin Laden family because they had *already* begun to plan a war against Afghanistan well before the events of 9/11. But they needed an excuse to do that (how convenient was 9/11?). The two authors allege that Bush (with the co-operation of Blair), attempted to bargain with the Taliban in Afghanistan, asking them to give up Osama bin Laden in return for political recognition and lots of economic aid. Apparently, the Taliban Ambassador to Pakistan (yes, they did have one) was told that, either you accept our offer of a carpet of gold, or we bury you under a carpet of bombs. It seems they chose the bombs.

They claim the US government needed to parley with the Taliban so it could gain access to the oil reserves and also construct a gas pipeline which avoided Russian territory, in peace. It is further alleged that the US threatened to attack as far back as 2001 during their negotiations to build a gas pipeline through Turkmenistan and Afghanistan to ports in Pakistan.

According to Peter Allen of the *Daily Mail*, one of President Bush's first business partners was bin Laden's eldest brother, Salem bin Laden. Allen has said, "In the 1970s, he (Salem bin Laden) and George H.W. Bush were founders of the Arbusto Energy oil company, in Bush's home state of Texas."

George Herbert Walker Bush and the bin Laden family had been connected via dubious business deals since Salem, head of the bin Laden family business – one of the biggest construction companies in the world – invested in Bush's start-up oil company Arbusto Energy Incorporated. James R. Bath, a friend and neighbour was used to funnel money from Osama bin Laden's brother Salem bin Laden to set up G.H.W. Bush in the oil business.

According to the *Wall Street Journal* and other reputable sources, such as the *Washington Post*, the Carlyle Group met at the Ritz Carlton Hotel in New York City one day before the events of 9/11. In attendance at this meeting were former president G.H.W. Bush and Shafiq bin Laden, another brother of Osama bin Laden. The Carlyle Group is a large private-equity investment firm, closely associated with officials of the Bush and Reagan administrations, and has considerable ties to Saudi oil money, including ties to the bin Laden family.

Through a truly tangled web of Saudi multi-millionaires and Texas oilmen, including the infamous Bank of Credit and Commerce International (BCCI), the ex-president was financially linked with the bin Laden family, until Salem met an untimely end by flying a British-made microlight into some power cables in 1988.

The Bank of Credit and Commerce was shut down in 1991, with some $10 billion in losses. Nevertheless, well before then, in June 1977, G.H.W. Bush formed his own oil drilling company, Arbusto Energy, in Midland, Texas. (Arbusto, which the Bush family wrongly interpreted as 'bush', actually means 'shrub' in Spanish.) According to the British *Daily Mail*, Salem bin Laden, who was a close friend of the Saudi King, Fahd, invested heavily in Bush's first business venture.

As I have said before (*or if I haven't, I'm saying it now*) it's about many things, including simple business acumen. But by the nature of man and of capitalism, it unfortunately includes manifold power; concerns about prestige; a seriously unhealthy love of money; personal ambition; a staggering lack of altruism and ethics; all on a monumental scale. It all too often includes, as in the case of Volkswagen, HSBC, and the Vatican Bank, outright fraud (see Chapter 7). But principally, it's about the coming power vacuum of a difficult to obtain, black, sticky, billion-year-old artefact, called oil.

*

In January 1976, President Chavez of Venezuela nationalised its oil wells, re-naming them Petróleos de Venezuela. Later, numerous deals were struck with other countries in attempts to get around dealing with the United States, which infuriated the White House. Deals were also struck to let thousands of Venezuelans receive medical treatment and health programs from Cuba; in return Venezuela agreed to sell several thousands of barrels to Cuba at a 40 percent discount. The US State Department was beside itself. This led to many attempts on the life of President Chavez.

Most notable was the 2002 coup d'état during which he was kidnapped and would have been assassinated, had it not been for an unprecedented uprising of the Venezuelan people and loyal military forces that rescued him and returned him to power within forty-eight hours. Irrefutable evidence emerged later, using the Freedom of Information Act, that the CIA and other agencies were behind the coup attempt and that they financially supported those involved. There were numerous further attempts against Chavez and his government that were backed by the CIA.

In 2004 dozens of Colombian paramilitaries were captured outside of Caracas on a farm owned by a notorious anti-Chavez activist, Robert Alonso. They were apprehended only one day before they were due to attack the presidential palace and kill Chavez. A lesser-known plot against Chavez was uncovered in New York, during his visit to the United Nations General Assembly in September 2006. During a standard reconnaissance by his own security service at a university venue, in which Chavez had been booked to address the students and various members of the public, high levels of radiation were found to be emanating from the chair on which he was due to sit.

The radiation was discovered by a Venezuelan security agent holding a hand-held Geiger counter. The chair was removed and subsequent tests showed it emitting levels of radiation more than sufficient to create significant harm, had it not been discovered. Chavez's own security at the university discovered that an individual from the US, who had been involved in the logistical support for the event, had provided and placed the chair. Later he was shown to have been acting for US Intelligence (an oxymoronic title if ever there was one). Chavez died in 2013 and arranged for a previous bus driver, Nicolás Maduro, to take his place. Through rampant and very obvious corruption his rule is about to end.

(It's okay for the CIA to play such games but Russia mustn't play any kind of cyber game – absolutely not cricket old boy. But in fact, Russia has just announced it has undetectable ICBMs that cannot be intercepted, plus underwater drones carrying nuclear weapons. Here we go again. In the meantime, Russia has contrived to kill or maim with a rare type of nerve agent, a former Russian commander who spied for Britain but was released in an exchange programme and lived in the very British town of Salisbury. A stupider act is difficult to imagine, but then nobody would call Putin or the FSB intellectuals. However, since the assassination of Trotsky in Mexico, they have killed and attempted to kill numerous times, including murdering the ex-FSB officer Alexander Litvinenko with polonium, and the assumed cross-dresser Gareth Williams, who worked for MI6 at GCHQ Cheltenham, and was apparently aware of a mole in GCHQ. The name of the game is power.)

Another thwarted attempt on the life of Chavezo occurred in July 2010. Francisco Chavez Abarca (no relation)was a low-life working with Cuban-born, ex-CIA-turned-terrorist, Luis Posada Carriles, the reptile responsible for killing seventy-three passengers on a Cuban airliner in 1976. Carriles was detained entering Venezuela and confessed he had been chosen via devious routes to assassinate Chavez.

The SVR (Russia's Foreign Intelligence Service) is clearly not alone in foreign assassination attempts. In February 2010while President Chavez was attending an event near the Colombian border, his security forces uncovered a sniper over a quarter of a mile away intent on shooting the president. He was – in the jargon of security services everywhere – officially neutralised.

Hugo Chavez's government led a socialist-type revolution using oil money to further education, health, and housing. There is little doubt he made some mistakes along the way. Nevertheless, he defied the powerful interests of the United States, consistently refusing to be their puppet-on-a-string. This won him very few friends in America, particularly as he was the head of a nation with the largest remaining oil reserves on the planet and someone who directly challenged US and Western domination of the oil-producing countries.

Chavez was considered very much a class enemy of the United States and was seen as a sort of latter-day Che Guevara. He was quoted at the 2005 World Social Forum as saying,

> "It is impossible, within the framework of the capitalist system to solve the grave problems of poverty of the majority of the world's population. We must transcend capitalism. But we cannot resort to state capitalism, which would be the same perversion as the Soviet Union. We must reclaim socialism as a thesis, a project and a path, a new type of socialism, a humanist one, which puts humans and not machines or the state ahead of everything. That's the debate we must promote around the world, and the World Social Forum, is a good place to do it."

He also famously called George Bush the Devil, and enemy number one.

So, let's be absolutely clear, shall we? The United States was out to get him because, amongst the alphabet soup of American intelligence agencies, the word *socialism* is tantamount to the words paedophile, festering sore, Marxism, Mexican, or shit on your shoes. Plus, the gentleman was sitting on more black gold than Croesus.

So, they got him!

At least, according to the journalist Wayne Madsen (who in my opinion is not to be entirely trusted, although he gets things right occasionally). After all, Madsen famously thought President Barack Obama was gay and born in Kenya, neither of which was shown to be true.

This 'journalist' has made it clear (to everyone who will listen) that he believes DNA has been collected by the CIA from every world leader in case they needed to whack him (or her). Then they would do so by making a disease specific to that person's DNA. To this end, they supposedly collected DNA from Chavez, from a restaurant glass, a barber shop, or something similar. Then, according to Madsen, they gave him cancer and he died on the 5 March 2015.Two presidents of Brazil close to Chavez, including the impeached Dilma Rousseff and President Lula, also developed cancer. In total, seven Latin American presidents developed highly aggressive, fast-acting cancer. "Not a coincidence," says Wayne Madsen.

The current Venezuelan president, who used to be the vice president, has propelled the country into hyper-inflation and poverty, with hundreds of thousands attempting to leave. In Brazil, the rise of the far right and the re-emerging military mentality has both ex-president Lula in prison and has swept Jair Bolsonaro into power, accompanied by 'Operation Carwash', the title for an operation theoretically cleansing Brazil of corruption: but presumably not of hypocrisy.

The scribbler Madsen, could be right of course, even though such a view of the external world is profoundly depressing and consistently marks the human race as having fallen on its face or, as the US military has yelled since the Second World War, 'FUBAR' (fucked up beyond any repair).

Do you by any chance remember the show South Pacific when the world was a very different place and people such as Wayne

Madsen did not exist – perhaps they didn't need to?

When the sky is a bright canary yellow
I forget every cloud I've ever seen,
So they called me a cockeyed optimist
Immature and incurably green.
I have heard people rant and rave and bellow
That we're done and we might as well be dead,
But I'm only a cockeyed optimist
And I can't get it into my head.
I hear the human race
Is fallin' on its face
And hasn't very far to go,
But every whippoorwill
Is sellin' me a bill,
And tellin' me it just ain't so.
I could say life is just a bowl of Jello
And appear more intelligent and smart,
But I'm stuck like a dope
With a thing called hope,
And I can't get it out of my heart!
Not this heart...

Associate professor Julia Steinberger, of the Faculty of Environment in Leeds University UK, has said,

> "Some of the strongest determinants of life satisfaction are good health, strong family and community relationships, economic security in the form of employment, and relative rather than absolute wealth with respect to the rest of one's society. There's a lot we can learn about how to move to lower material forms of life satisfaction. We can no longer pretend that simply letting the market decide what is best for us will lead to anything but disaster. We would argue that material de-growth of the richest nations is imperative for medium and long-term planetary stability."

One step, in countries that are already considered wealthy, may be to stop judging progress by economic measures like 'gross domestic product'. What really matters, are health, happiness, meaningful employment, and equality (*New Scientist,* 10 February 2018, p10).

Mark Nelson is the founding director of the Institute of Eco-technics in Santa Fe, New Mexico. He has, with seven others, lived in a biosphere bubble, simply called 'Biosphere 2' for two years in a brave attempt to imitate Biosphere 1 (the Earth).

This pre-Martian experiment initially experienced some difficulties, particularly with controlling carbon dioxide, but was eventually successful. Afterwards he said the following,

> "The biosphere experience showed me how urgently we need to change our paradigms for living on Earth, that we are not separate from nature... It showed me that we need engineers to redesign our techno sphere, so that we can stop destroying our beautiful Earth and begin regenerating it. And also, that we need artists and writers and thinkers to help create a spiritual and cultural awakening, one that will allow us to become effective stewards, not only of our planet, but also ourselves."

The best unspecific criticism of the mindless idiots in the White House has to be, as the famous American journalist and satirist, H.L. Mencken, once said, a long time ago,

> "There is always a well-known solution to every human problem – neat, plausible, ***and wrong!***"

*

If you think none of this applies to the European Union: think again. The EU Home Affairs Commissioner Cecilia Malmstroem, has pointed out that the corruption figure in the EU is actually far higher than the estimated £120 billion... (*£120, 000,000,000*)

"The extent of the problem in Europe is breathtaking, although Sweden is among the countries with the least problems. The cost to the EU economy is equivalent to the bloc's annual budget."

A previous whistle blower in 2000, Robert Mcoy, became aware of staggering, almost unbelievable systematic fraudulent claims on expenses. He was summarily dismissed. Then castigated as being anti-European, including, on numerous occasions, having his family threatened during anonymous midnight phone calls.

You can't think of a good reason for the UK leaving the EU? I just gave you one!

CHAPTER 2

"The concept of global warming was created by the Chinese in order to make US manufacturing non-competitive."

President Donald Trump

The oil business is a strange business, and a very, very secretive one. Countries do not like to admit how much oil they have in reserve and traditionally exaggerate the amount. The oil companies themselves also do this. This exacerbates the difficulties in estimating how much oil remains in reserves underground, and how much has been stockpiled for the end-game. There appear to be four separate opinions or voices doing the rounds and all four voices are contradictory.

Voice One:

The most loudly spoken and confident opinion, the one that governments tend to listen to, comes from conventional free market economists who view energy as simply another product. Therefore, this 'product' is subject to the same market forces as any other, and is consequently prone to temporary shortages which cause the price to rise, thus stimulating more production which, in turn, eventually lowers the price (*after a fat profit has been made*). So, to them, the ups and downs are simply market imperfections that often result from 'government regulations'. But the market itself always eventually recovers, assuming it is not hampered by 'price caps' and other forms of 'government regulations'. This voice has almost nothing at all to say about the future decline, or global warming engendered by fossil fuels. It is simply a (deluded) economist's voice.

Voice Two:

The Green opinion: the environmental activists who are concerned about the build-up of greenhouse gasses and the over-sized carbon footprint left by humanity remorselessly stepping on the world. They are particularly concerned with hydrocarbons and the obvious pollution taking place on and in the sea and the atmosphere, such as plastics which are gradually destroying the eco-system. These types of concerned people are often (but not exclusively) on the Left, politically. They are in consummate favour of renewable energy sources: windmills, tidal stream generators, wave generators, solar panels, bio-fuels, etc. Some of them (a few) admit that nuclear power might be the answer, assuming a cleaner and safer method can be found. This group, although very naïve about the saving grace of renewable sources, are at least trying to ensure our environment is liveable for our children and grandchildren and they should be listened to.

Voice Three:

The truth tellers, the whistle-blowers, the concerned (commonly) retired and independent petroleum geologists, who can see the advancing catastrophic tsunami all too clearly, and are trying to say so, amidst a cacophony of unconcerned 'live-now-pay-later' bunkum, baloney and poppycock. These geologists have complete contempt for the 'Voice One' economists; and rightly so, because economists reduce all material resources to dollars and graphs, as if nothing else matters. The economists' view obscures the real physical issues involved, and is, in the opinion of the whistle–blowers, extremely dangerous. They agree with the Voice Two Greens that alternative energy sources are necessary, but they do not agree that they will replicate oil – *or come even close*. And at the present construction and quantities involved of windmills, solar panels, etc., decades of production will be needed to produce sufficient energy to provide one fifth of what oil presently produces. And, of course, windmills, wave generators and solar panels cannot fly aeroplanes nor navigate ocean liners and cargo ships across the Atlantic (but sail power and or hydrogen cells might). They also cannot make double-glazed windows, computer printers, phones, or TVs. Eventually, some alternatives might be found for this application of oil, such as wood-based, fibre-based, or vegetable-based materials. But if so, they need to start experimenting now.

(New Scientist 16 March 2018 p33, has an article by Graham Lawton, pointing out that in the not-too-distant future, the need to stop using concrete, steel, and all forms of plastic, will ensure that all buildings and all transport will be made from wood. Not quite wood as we currently know it: but wood nevertheless. This technology has already produced a cross-laminated building material called CLT, which will be used to construct an 80-story, 300 metre high, tower-block, right in the middle of London's Barbican Centre.)

Voice Four:

The voice of the actual decision makers: politicians. *Now we are in trouble.* As previously argued, politicians are ordinary folk; they are not normally specialists in what matters to, or in, the world at large. Business studies, or even a degree with honours in mining, will not even begin to teach or to indicate that the oil is running out, or that the gas is running out, or that effectively the entire energy source of the world is running out. I once asked my daughter, who is completing a Master's Degree in mining, if, during her entire university course, a single word was mentioned about the finite qualities of the minerals, metals, and fossil fuels they were teaching them to mine. "No," she said. "The unspoken assumption by most tutors is they will last for hundreds of years, or at least, so far into the future that various viable alternatives for all of them will be found." And that is exactly the concept carried in the hearts-and- minds of most politicians, because it's easier to believe that, than to face the truth. Politicians are gullible (and remember they are not geologists), so they will believe the economists (such as Dieter Helm) because it's an acceptable message and no politician wants to have to say, 'Ladies and gentlemen we have some very good news and some very bad news. The good news is we are going to tell the absolute truth for a change. The bad news is, the age of cheap oil, of motor cars and planes and ships, is coming to an end, and the two principal energy sources that run the entire world, oil and gas, will run out before your kids have kids.' So, they won't say it or anything appertaining to it. And who's listening to the retired and independent geologists? Just about nobody I suspect: certainly *not* Professor Dieter Helm.

*

Part of the good news could be that, simply by accident, in a post-petroleum world, humans will discover a way of life that is less frantic, much closer to home and ecologically sustainable – meaning happier. You won't necessarily be able to take a world cruise anymore (unless sixty to 100 years from now, you travel on a hydrogen or bio-powered ship) but you might be able to sail your engineless boat around it. You won't be able to catch a diesel train to work, but you might be able to cycle there. You won't be able to drive 400 or more miles on a holiday in your caravan or camper, but you might be able to roller skate down the deserted motorways and camp on the grass fringes; this assumes that crime on a grand scale does not replace law and order, meaning doing such a thing would be taking your life in your hands.

One thing seems certain, based on many oil men's and geologists' opinions. Within your child's lifetime, the oil and gas will run out. The Industrial Revolution, which began in Britain and gradually spread to the rest of the world, will stagger to a climatic ending and, with luck, because of the late industri-alisation of the developing world it will run out a lot sooner than expected. I say *luck,* because the sooner we face up to this calamity and learn to live with its consequences, the better off the remaining population will be.

And I say *remaining,* because unless we approach this certainty with the correct attitude and have already applied as much sci-ence as we can muster to the global warming problem, deadly chaos will ensue. The remaining oil will be more expensive than gold, so vehicles will not be delivering food to the super-markets anymore by this method. There may be a viable WTE product or fuel cell alternative that is only available to elec-tric/oil supermarket delivery vehicles, and similarly to police vehicles. It will still be very, very expensive, so food prices will skyrocket.

Many people will not be able to sustain their mortgages because getting to work will be virtually impossible or incredibly ex-pensive; the government will not be able to pay sustainable un-employment benefit, because there will be millions of people affected, so homelessness will be rampant. No work, no home, no income, and no central heating or air conditioning is a recipe for an unprecedented crime wave.

Preppers (the derogatory name given to survivalists) in the US, think they are going to live sustainable lives if a nuclear attack, a revolution, or any kind of civil disturbance takes place. But all too often these same preppers rely on diesel generators to oper-ate their air supply or their electricity, and petroleum for their chain saws. Nevertheless, they have the right idea and may sur-vive longer than most, possibly long enough to help start a new way of life in their given area. But in the cities people will expire by violence or starvation in the millions. But rather strangely, among what is considered by many people the brightest and the best of the first world countries on this benighted planet, the United States of America seems to be leading this headlong charge into degradation and oblivion, before anyone else, well before it happens because of the lack of oil.

Maybe they're practising. (See Chapters 10 and 11.)

Is this too bleak a view of the future? Well maybe – just maybe – something will save us; something will come along, such as Manchester's hydrogen fuel cell breakthrough, or waste to energy biomass. The possibility does exist. But it's slimmer than my bank balance.

The American military are also working on varieties of energy garnered from the understanding of particle physics using quantum theory possibilities (such as the Casimir effect) and such energy is also remotely possible. But even if that is the case and such an energy source exists (or will exist) and is usable, they will use it to sustain themselves in the final conflicts over the last of the oil. You and yours are very unlikely to get anywhere near it.

Meanwhile WTE sources or vegetable oils might act as the necessary lubricant in any given machinery. But if that is the case, it needs to be brought to fruition now. Not twenty years from now, not ten or five, but right NOW!

And the truth is, if you explore the current field of so-called alternative energies, only a few are viable in any sort of quantity. There are twelve alternatives to oil and gas. They are as follows.

1) Biofuel

2) Biomass (including WTE)

3) Geothermal

4) Hydropower

5) Tidal power

6) Solar energy

7) Wave power

8) Wind power

9) Radiant energy

10) Nuclear energy

11) Hydrogen cell energy

12) Human energy, or slave energy.

Leaving out (for the moment) historical human slave energy, all eleven would have to be used to full capacity to equal the energy trapped in oil. All of them except two are designed to eventually generate electricity, which is an energy carrier, not energy of itself. Only one is a lubricant.

Synthetic oil is currently made from chemicals and petroleum. It would surely be possible to make it fully synthetic and not use petroleum? Possibly bio-fuel oil, such as olive oil, could be substituted, but it would be very expensive when needed in large quantities. It's pretty dammed expensive now.

But just think of all the machinery in the world which needs metal-to-metal lubrication on a moment-to-moment basis.

All mineral oils and synthetic oils are based on petroleum or oil derivatives. Solid lubricants (such as the PTFEs in your frying pan) are insufficiently capable of high friction, although they can withstand heat. Inorganic solids, such as graphite, boron nitride, molybdenum disulphide and tungsten disulphide are poorly resistant to oxidation.

Metal/alloys and pure metals can be used as grease additives, or sometimes act as the sole constituents of sliding surfaces and bearings. Cadmium and gold give good sliding surfaces (if somewhat expensive). Lead, zinc and bronze, are also excellent bearing surfaces, or their powders can be used as a lubricant.

Aqueous lubrication, such as strongly hydrated brush polymers (PEG), can act as an efficient lubricant at liquid-solid interfaces. Bio-lubricants (triglyceride esters) are fats obtained from plants and animals and even WTE. Another naturally derived lubricant is lanolin, derived from sheep wool.

All of these lubricant possibilities could be worked on and improved for worldwide machine lubrication, but all current machines need oil or petroleum or gas to work in the first place – and there is still no real and viable substitute on the immediate horizon for any of these: and even if there were, what do you think the oil moguls would do?

*

Five thousand one hundred thirty-five US patents have been confiscated under National Security orders. If you invented genuinely free energy tomorrow, the only way you might keep it afloat is if you made no part of it secret and let social media know about it and the way it worked from day one. But you would be surprised how difficult even that is. The patent could still be seized on the excuse that it undermines national security. Meaning it rocks the military/industrial complex's boat.

Is there any such a thing as free energy that does not contradict the first law of thermodynamics? Apparently, there is! A calculator and/or a weather station can be run from the spare microwaves emanating from a TV broadcasting tower, as long as it's in line of sight. Broadcasting microwave towers push out vast quantities of radio frequency (RF), hoping that it will hit a TV antenna and ensure that Mr and Mrs Smith can still watch Coronation Street, or find some other way to avoid hard international questions and personal truths.

Demands on such power at the antenna are less than they were in the past. This means that much of the spare RF, acting as a current in a stream, can manage to turn the digital wheels inside any small electronic device. Whatever technology is pumping out the RF, such as a TV station, cell tower, or a home Wi-Fi system, never actually feels the extra draw because of the free-floating radio frequencies that simply didn't make it to the intended location, wherever that is. This is of course, more like *freely available*, than genuine free energy. Another more advanced technology is a Wireless Resonant Energy Link, demonstrated in 2007, in which a 40-watt light bulb is kept lit, at one metre away from its RF source.

Free energy devices have apparently been demonstrated many times throughout history, often using magnets, such as the Mike Brady magnetic motor and the pinwheel gravity engine, plus the plastic fan with small magnets on the blades that spin when a much stronger magnet is drawn close. This method can be used to light a bulb and *appears* to display genuine free energy, which could, in theory, be geared up to run an entire generating station. Many of the gimmicks shown on YouTube simply don't work. But one or two *do* appear to work –and effectively you only need one genuine device. We are not talking about renewable energy here. Free energy is only ever semi-permanent, because nothing can violate the 'second law of thermodynamics'. Entropy will still bring the entire construction to an ignominious and grinding full stop, without constant upgrading, renewal, and maintenance.

A more recent biologically free energy discovery has been made by Anirvan Guha, et al., at the University of Fribourg, in Switzerland, based on how electric eels work. Thousands of hydrogel bubbles were spread across a thin pliable surface with a second sheet placed on top and the gap filled with a saline solution. The ions in the salt water caused friction between the two layers and generated electricity in the gel layers, providing an unbelievable 110 volts. The university is looking for a forty-fold improvement and a higher current. The system is designed to provide continuous battery free electricity (*New Scientist*, 24 Feb 2018, p18).

In 1948 the Dutch Physicist Hendrick Casimir discovered a force in quantum field theory now called the Casimir effect. To understand the Casimir effect, one has to understand how the vacuum of space is viewed in quantum field theory.

Space is not empty. Contemporary physicists assume that the so-called vacuum of space is full of fluctuating electromagnetic waves that cannot be completely eliminated, similar to the waves in the oceans, which are always present and can never truly be stopped. These waves fluctuate across every possible wavelength, implying that empty space contains energy that is ever present.

To demonstrate this, scientists placed two mirrors (or plates) fairly close together facing each other in a vacuum. Some of the above waves just fitted between the mirrors, bouncing backward and forward off the surface like ping-pong balls. If, during the experiment, the two mirrors are moved even closer together, the longer waves will not now fit into the gap. This means that the amount of energy in the vacuum between the plates is fractionally less than the amount everywhere outside. The effect is that the two mirrors tend to attract each other in the same way that two objects held apart by a taut spring will move gradually together as the energy stored in the spring is decreased.

Steve K. Lamoreaux, now at Los Alamos National Laboratory, initially measured the minute force involved in 1996. He discovered that if the mirrors are moved rapidly, some of the vacuum waves become real waves. It has been suggested that this dynamical Casimir effect is responsible for the mysterious phenomenon known as sonluminescence: the curious emission of short bursts of light from imploding bubbles in a liquid when it is excited by sound.

Scientific theory considers that the amount of energy in any given piece of a vacuum can be altered by the material around it, and the term Casimir effect is also used in this broader context. Vacuum energy is fascinating, in that, when calculated in quantum field theory it is infinite and could, if developed correctly, be an enormous source of free energy, known as 'zero point' energy.

The problem would seem to be that an infinite vacuum energy does not agree with Einstein's theory of gravitation, which states that such an energy source would produce an infinite gravitational curvature of space-time. This cannot be observed in practise. No resolution has yet been found. But even if it were, how long do you think it would take for such an energy source to be fully recognised and used: one hundred years, two hundred years – maybe a lot longer?

The truth is: we cannot rely on exotic processes to solve the energy shortage problem. We simply don't have the time. We have to make the energy sources we know and understand work now, work quicker, and work more effectively, while at the same time reducing the amount of escaped noxious gasses we are pumping into the atmosphere. It's not the tallest of tall orders; we have faced similar tall orders. Defeat Nazi Germany. Defeat Imperialist Japan. And defeat world recession. To combat these problems, we used every idea we could think of, from bailing out banks, to successful code breaking, to beach ball shaped bouncing bombs, to welded ships, to radar and finally atomic bombs.

We can combat global warming and the subsequent loss of fossil fuels in the same determined manner. But we need to work together and to place all the best brains on the subject. Meanwhile America needs to stop this ludicrous denial nonsense exacerbated by the scientifically ignorant Republican Christian Right.

CHAPTER 3

"Oil depletion and climate change will create an entirely new context in which political struggles will be played out. Within that context, it is not just freedom, democracy, and equality that are at stake, but the survival of billions of humans and of whole ecosystems."

Richard Heinberg, writer and journalist

Let us for a moment travel back to the Dark Ages, that long mysterious sparsely populated period between the ninth and the fourteenth centuries, when there was no healthcare of any kind, no welfare, no electric light, no fridges, no radio or TV and no community charge either.

All historians agree that this period could be defined as one of sustained growth in Europe. Initially under the Roman yoke, the populations increased and urbanisation quickly spread, due to the formation of numerous small towns and villages and an increase in the numbers of inhabitants of the older conurbations.

During the same period an understanding of technical abilities was greatly improved and procedural changes brought about a marked material progress of the European world. Were we able to travel back in time and take a helicopter ride over the European mainland, not only would we create instant heart attacks in the terrified inhabitants – who would think God or Jesus had arrived – but we would also observe a huge forest stretching as far as the eye could see.

In clearings we would just be able to discern thatched huts made of mud and wattle with smoke rising from wood fires. Occasionally we might observe a somewhat larger conurbation, clearly about to become a small town, and there we might observe the technologies of the age being made: a wooden plough, a wooden cart with oak wooden wheels, a wine-press, a spinning-wheel.

As we flew over a fairly large nearby lake, we might see wooden fishing boats in the process of net fishing. Wood was the dominant construction material, often held together with iron or even copper nails. Wood was also the dominant energy source. Charcoal, made from slowly burning wood under heaps of turf, was used to fire up furnaces and smelt metals. If you could maintain your health and avoid the plague (easier in the country) this was in many ways an idyllic lifestyle. And if you could not, cunning women (sometimes referred to as witches) would know exactly which plant balm to apply to alleviate the symptoms of ordinary bacterial and viral conditions.

Wood, particularly oak, was abundant, ever plentiful, and burnt with a sustaining heat. You didn't have to pay a haulier to deliver the stuff to your shed or garden; you simply walked into the woods and chopped down a tree or two. And of course, a profusion of wild animals lay near your doorstep such as deer, boar, and edible birds, such as quail, duck, geese and pheasant. Many people kept chickens and pigs and traded the eggs and meat as a palatable dish mixed with split or pulverised acorns.

The population of Europe during the time of Charlemagne amounted to approximately thirty million, and of the UK, just over two million. The priests of the Celtic tribes of Europe, including what is now called the United Kingdom, were known as Druids and worshipped the oak groves and tree spirits. But with the gradual infiltration of Christianity, and as the political boundaries of the Roman Empire diminished and then finally collapsed in the West, Christianity spread beyond the old borders of the Empire and into lands that had never been under the rule of Rome.

The fifth century saw a unique culture develop around the Irish Sea, consisting of what is now called Wales and Ireland. Christianity spread from Roman Britain to Ireland due to the missionary zeal of Saint Patrick and his apparent ability to dispense with snakes. Saint Patrick had originally been forced into slavery in Ireland and eventually managed to escape. Later he became consecrated as a bishop, and returned to the isle that had enslaved him, so that he could convert the people to Christianity.

Missionary priests initially ordained by him accompanied him to Ireland. Soon Irish missionaries spread his type of Christianity, with its particularly Irish features, to Scotland and the Continent. One notable feature was a system of private penitence, which replaced the former practice of penance as a public rite.

By 407 CE, the Roman legions had left Britain and the Roman elite soon followed. Later that century barbarian tribes had finally upgraded their violent life-style from raiding and pillaging Britain, to settling down and invading other areas. These were known as the Anglo-Saxon tribes and were the predecessors of the English (the Welsh, the Irish, and the Scots are, or were, originally Celts).

The Anglo Saxons, having never been part of the Roman Empire, were entirely and completely pagan, and although well aware of the Christian influences surrounding them, were generally considered unconvertible. That is, until Pope Gregory the Great sent St Augustine to enthusiastically wave his magic wand. But even then, it finally took an enterprising Archbishop named Theodore, to ensure that the Anglo-Saxon tribes were finally and incontrovertibly converted to Christianity. This led to a long period of peace, culture, and scholarship, which itself eventually led to the conversion of France, then of the lowlands, and finally all of Europe.

*

A few hundred years later, the human life style and energy source in Europe had stopped being so idyllic. It was no longer supplied by individuals, families, or small communities – *à partir de*, a log cabin in the wilderness. The population had become a combination of what we would now call slaves or indentured peasants, relieved in their labour only by oxen. In Spain and France mules were also added to the mix and provided motive power for agriculture and transport. Wood still remained the principal fuel.

Around the twelfth century horses came on the scene. They had obviously been around for a long time as riding mounts for the cavalry and for medieval knights, but had not previously been used in large quantities for farm work such as tilling the land. The improved horse collar and the improved plough soon altered that situation.

A horse needs four or five acres of grass to be fed properly. That's a lot of land not being used for growing crops, and so a trade-off existed between the horses over oxen advantages, against those of lost arable land. Originally only the wealthiest could afford such a luxury. However, by 1900 Britain had a horse population of over three million, consuming four million tons of oats and hay every year, necessitating large imports of grain.

The medieval period saw both human and animal power supplemented by windmills and water mills. Water mills were universal and had been used by the Chinese for centuries, but Roman Britain had witnessed the technology improved considerably. Such Roman expertise was not lost on the Anglo-Saxons, who employed water wheels and windmills in very innovative and clever ways, such as using gears to harness the wheels' energy to operate saws and grinding stones, to pump water from the earliest coal mines, and to eventually crush ores, make wood-pulp paper and to forge iron.

The use of wood as the principal energy source continued apace, until the forests looked from the air as if they suffered from serious alopecia, and forest dwellers could no longer chop down their own trees. Consequently, the price of wood began to soar. Between 400 CE and 1600 CE, the forest cover in Europe was reduced from 95 percent to 20 percent. The shortages, plus the increasing price, pushed the price of other goods beyond reach, and starvation stalked the towns and cities of Britain and Europe.

(When the principal energy source (or sources) is/are removed from any society or any lifestyle, anywhere on the planet, history shows that starvation and death quickly follow.)

Energy source depletion led populations to consider a fuel that was previously recognised and occasionally had been used, but was considered dirty and, even then, unhealthy and very acidic with a choking bitter smoke: coal.

Coal, the first fossil fuel, was one of man's earliest sources of heat and light, and in the Forest of Dean in Gloucestershire, where numerous, small, bell-like coal pits still survive; it was used to complement wood throughout the Middle Ages. The Chinese were known to have used it more than three thousand years ago. In the New World, coal was discovered by French explorers on the Illinois River in 1679, and the earliest recorded commercial mining occurred near Richmond, Virginia in 1748.

In Britain during the Roman Empire, the Romans used coal obtained from drift mines and bell pits for heating their bathing pools and for the under- floor heating of villas. By the second century they were trading it along the North Sea coast and even over to continental Europe. Coal stores have even been found at many places along Hadrian's Wall.

After the collapse of the Roman Empire coal was not much heard of until the twelfth century, when monks began mining it for the smelting of iron. The artisanal over use of coal in London created considerable pollution, and in 1306 a Royal Proclamation was issued prohibiting artisans from using coal in their furnaces, commanding them to return to wood and charcoal. Coal pollution would remain a problem in London for another seven hundred years.

In the eighteen hundreds, the annual world coal output stood at fifteen million tons. By 1900 it had shot to 700 million tons a year, an increase of 4,000 percent. It continued to increase until coal gas and natural gas began to gradually replace it as an energy source.

Coal is now, in the United Kingdom, at its lowest use since the nineteenth century. The use of coal to generate electricity has halved and we have the lowest carbon pollution since 1894, apart from coal mining disputes in the 1920s.

Emissions of carbon dioxide (CO_2) have fallen by 50 percent and fossil fuel use overall has dropped by 52 percent as a result of higher carbon taxes and cheap gas, plus the expansion of renewable energy sources and the closure of three coal-fired power stations, at Longannet, Ferrybridge and Rugely.

Nevertheless, 7 percent of the UKs electrical energy is still supplied by a coal-fired power station situated at Drax, in Selby, Yorkshire, in which flue-gas desulphurisation was fitted between 1988 and 1999, earning it the title of the cleanest power station in Europe to produce 3,960 megawatts.

Regardless of that, it is still the largest producer of carbon dioxide in the UK. It burns thirty thousand tons of coal a day, obtained, not from South Wales, but from South Africa and Siberia. In fact, it emits more carbon dioxide than all of Sweden, and more than all the aircraft entering and leaving Heathrow in a year. Attempts to introduce carbon capture and storage (CCS) have failed due to lack of government subsidies.

Gas is now the principal energy source used for heating homes and generating electricity, although its use has fallen recently and now stalled somewhat, due to better insulation and improved gas boilers (New Scientist, 6 March, 2017). The world gets a quarter of its energy from natural gas, the consumption of which has doubled in the last thirty years. The forecasts are that it will double again quite soon as developing nations come on line.

Nevertheless, it is finite. The ExxonMobil Vice President, Harry J. Longwell, has placed the global peak during the mid-1970s, and has observed a sharp decline since then in gas discovery. The rate of discovery fell below the rate of consumption in 1980, and the gap has been widening ever since.

Despite the reported fall in new-field discoveries, reserves of natural gas have continued to grow from nineteen billion cubic metres in 1960, to forty-five billion cubic metres in 1970, and eighty-four billion cubic metres in 1980, to a record high of 200 billion cubic metres in 2012. This occurs because of better technology in withdrawal and additional gas pockets found within existing fields. But it is just as finite as oil and is set to run out only a few years later.

Effectively, what that means is that there is little new gas being discovered, nowhere near enough to keep up with current consumption, but they are getting better and better at scraping the barrel to use what we already have. The drawback is we simply mustn't use all that remains anyway...

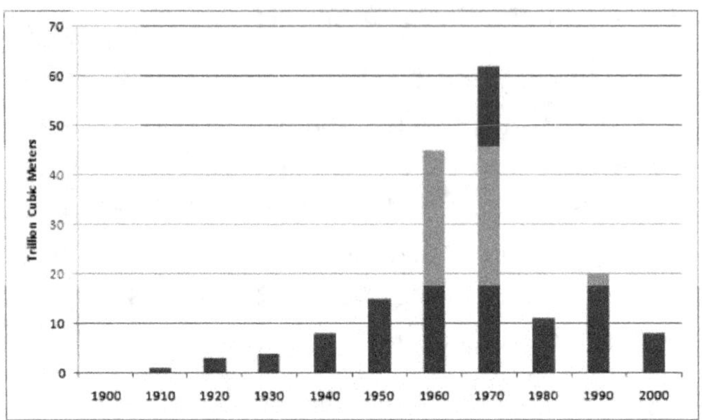

Note how, after the gas *discoveries* (not gas extraction) peaked in 1970 it was only ten years before it plunged to just over ten trillion cubic metres discovered in 1980, but recovered somewhat in 1990. This graph only takes us to 2000; since then discoveries have been minimal.

Here is the crucial factor: if the world burned all of its currently known reserves (without the use of CCS technology), we would emit a total of nearly 750 billion tonnes of carbon into the atmosphere. This fact alone means we need to leave around two-thirds of the known reserves in the ground if we want to meet our global climate targets as set by the Paris agreement.

For example, if we wanted to increase the probability of keeping global warming below two degrees Celsius (the standard set by the Paris agreement) to an 80 percent success rate, we would need much stricter carbon limits and would have to leave, coincidentally, 80 percent of the currently available fossil fuels untouched in the ground.

This means that, strictly speaking, we should not run to the end of production with any of these fuels, *not one of them.* So, the fact that with the coming developing world's demands, fossil fuels will run out in thirty to forty years (as a maximum) is simply academic. We can't really afford to continue to use them. lest we cook ourselves to a crisp or drown in our own beds.

These are just some of the alternatives we are facing.

But we *are* faced with them and what, exactly, are we doing about it? Well, just like the attitudes outlined on the first page of this book: very little. Instead we spend our energies and our political expertise (such as it is) on preserving the status quo, stupid foreign wars, Brexit problems and concerns about the fluff in our navels.

As first noted in the 'Introduction'.

Human beings are not just fallible, not just cock-up artists magnifique, they are covetous of the facts, protective of their own interests, concerned with their own infallibility and of course on many occasions, outright liars. The consequence is, little changes, and when it does, it has all too often been thought through by an aide to an aide with a degree in obfuscation.

It's damned unfortunate that this is true, because it means my kids and grandkids along with your kids and grandkids will suffer greatly. Not just because these fossil fuels are running out and we should be seriously restricting their use, but because there are no alternatives that apparently work, except nuclear for electricity and perhaps hydrogen fuel cells for cars, trains, planes and boats. But – to borrow the question in the Fermi paradox – where the hell are they?

Well, so far, they are in *one* experimental plane and *one* experimental ship (not yet actually built) and a few cars such as the Toyota Mirai, the Hyundai ix 35 and the Honda Clarity, although several other manufacturers are working on the technology.

The drawback is that 95 percent of hydrogen is currently made from natural gas or coal. Thus, making it produces very high carbon emissions, higher than manufacturing any type of petroleum product. The entire process has a huge capital cost burden, low energy content per unit volume, and we still lack the necessary technology to compress the highly volatile gas and make it truly safe. On top of which, the huge investment in infrastructure required to fuel vehicles on the roadside will take many years to bring about in order to avoid the no-fuel years, which are surely coming (unless, as previously suggested, it can be drawn from atmosphere).

It is possible to produce hydrogen from natural or renewable sources, such as geo-thermal. Iceland (along with Sweden) expects to be the first country in the world to be entirely hydrogen driven, in that its cars, its fishing fleet and home heating systems will all be hydrogen driven in fifty to sixty years. Two problems remain however. Currently the process is mind-bendingly expensive and – if the peak oil people are correct – *sixty years is much too late*. And Iceland thinks it will be the first, meaning that at least a third of a lifetime will be lived without adequate energy.

Not a lot of use, then!

But it might be – way, way into the future: particularly if notice is taken of the aforementioned Manchester discovery of the two-dimensional permeable matrix which might be able to extract hydrogen from the atmosphere. Trouble is, we are not looking way into the future. We are looking thirty-four years *or a lot less* into the future.

*

Current fuel cell cars and trucks combine hydrogen and oxygen to produce electricity, which then runs an electric motor. Fuel cell vehicles are usually considered electric vehicles but, unlike other electric vehicles, their driving range and refuelling process are similar to a conventional car or truck.

Converting hydrogen gas into electricity produces only water and heat as by-products, meaning fuel cell vehicles don't create tailpipe pollution when they're actually driven. However, producing the hydrogen from fossil gas produces massive pollution, as well as substantial greenhouse gas emissions. Yet even when the fuel comes from such a dirty source as natural gas, today's fuel cell cars and trucks manage to cut emissions by 30 percent when compared with their gasoline-powered counterparts.

Refuelling a contemporary fuel cell vehicle is comparable to refuelling a conventional car or truck. Pressurised hydrogen is sold at hydrogen refuelling stations, taking less than ten minutes to fill current models. Once filled, the driving ranges of fuel cell vehicles can vary, but are similar to the range of gasoline or diesel vehicles (200–300 miles). Compared to battery-driven electric vehicles, which are obliged to recharge their batteries by plugging in to the mains – they are a gift. (See previous charging problems.)

The combination of fast centralised refuelling and longer driving ranges makes fuel cells particularly appropriate for larger vehicles with long-distance requirements, or for drivers who lack plug-in access at home. ITM Power has several hydrogen refuelling stations situated throughout the UK. Like other EVs, fuel cell cars and trucks can employ 'idle off' which shuts down the fuel cell at traffic lights, stop signs, or in heavy traffic. In certain driving modes regenerative braking is used to capture lost energy and charge the battery or batteries.

Battery-driven electric vehicles run off an electric motor and a battery or batteries, which, like fuel cell vehicles, allow them to drive emissions-free, at least, when the electricity itself comes from renewable sources. Unlike fuel cell cars and trucks, battery electric vehicles can use the existing infrastructure to recharge their batteries, but must be plugged in for extended periods of time. (*Lithium batteries if finally extended to cover all aspects of ground-travel-transport, means lithium itself, has a mining life of twenty years.*)

Plug-in hybrid electric vehicles are similar to battery electric vehicles, but also use a conventional gasoline or diesel engine. This allows them to drive short distances on electricity, switching to a fossil fuel for longer trips. Although not as clean as a battery electric vehicle or a fuel cell vehicle, plug-in hybrids produce significantly less pollution than their conventional counterparts.

Conventional hybrids also have conventional engines and an electric motor and batteries; however, they cannot be plugged in. Though cleaner than conventional cars and trucks, non-plug-in hybrids derive their power to charge the batteries from their own gasoline or diesel engine, coupled with regenerative braking and therefore aren't considered an electric vehicle (Union of Concerned Scientists. www.ucsusa.org).

*

There is plenty of hydrogen; it's the most abundant element in the entire universe and it's inert at room temperature. In fact, it comprises 75 percent of all baryonic mass (normal atomic matter). No problem there then. *Except there is!*

Currently, obtaining hydrogen from pollution-producing natural gas and making it usable uses more energy than it puts out. Nevertheless, it's still a great alternative for cars, trucks, and maybe, someday, trains. But will it work in ships or planes? (If the new Manchester technology ever gets off the ground it will kick the current outdated hydrogen technology into touch surprisingly quickly, as long as some backward-thinking government schmuck doesn't make a huge fuss about free energy.)

Yes, it will work in ships and planes. In fact, if liquefied, it can be used in jet aircraft as a replacement propellant, or used via a hydrogen cell to power a propeller. It is, however, difficult to produce and very expensive. Also, even though it is one third the weight of kerosene, it is four times the volume and so needs a huge aircraft to carry the necessary voluminous tanks involved. It is also extremely volatile, and so needs to be carried in special pressurised tanks in the main body of the aircraft, not in the wings.

The Russian plane manufacturer Tupelev has already experimented with a hydrogen-fuelled plane: the TU-155 made a maiden flight in 1989. More recently, in July 2010, Boeing unveiled an unmanned test drone, called the Phantom Eye UAV, using two Ford internal combustion engines converted to operate on hydrogen. It was tested numerous times at several different altitudes and locations but was never put into production. It remains today in a military museum.

In 2011, an AeroVironment Global Observer was fitted with a hydrogen-fuelled propulsion system, becoming the world's first passenger aircraft with an engine powered by a hydrogen fuel cell. Its first flight took place in Stuttgart Airport, Germany, on 29 September 2016. It carried nine kilograms in weight, 4x11 kilowatt hydrogen fuel cells, and 2x20 kilowatt-hour batteries. It flew successfully, and a few are being manufactured as unmanned, long-distance, drone-type aircraft for military use.

Various versions of this technology are the most promising so far to replace petroleum or diesel in the future. But much experimental work has to be done to make them into passenger aircraft – *and there is so little time to do it.*

*

Viking Cruises have joined the ranks of shipping companies *talking* about fuel cell technology, with the announcement in June 2018 of plans to build the world's first cruise ship fuelled by liquid hydrogen. Project manager Serge Fossati told a shipping conference in Norway that the ship will be around 230 metres long and will accommodate more than 900 passengers and carry a crew of 500.

She will be based on the design of the cruise lines' other ocean-going ships, such as the Viking Sun. Several specially modified tenders to carry the fuel to the cruise ship are also part of the project. In the pipeline (so to speak) are several plans to build ferries and cargo ships based on hydrogen power. But that's where about 99 percent of these ideas are – *in the pipeline*. Currently the world's cargo vessels push out more CO_2 than all of Germany.

So far, liquid hydrogen itself has *not* been used as a marine fuel. A fuel cell converts the hydrogen to electricity for propulsion at the propeller and for electric power on board. A fuel cell power pack consists of a fuel and gas processing system and a stack of fuel cells that convert the chemical energy of the fuel to electric power through an electrochemical reaction.

The process can be described as similar to that of a battery with electrochemical reactions occurring at the interface between the anode or cathode and the electrolyte membrane, but with a continuous fuel and air supply. Different fuel cell types are available and can be characterised by the differing materials used in the membrane. One of the technical challenges is to maintain the liquid hydrogen at minus 250 degrees Celsius, to keep it from evaporating. Hydrogen is also a very explosive gas and protection against gas leaks is an important part of the safety requirements for the fuel (note the Hindenburg).

This Norwegian ship has been called a world sensation, and it is exciting. If the vessel works as it should, a distribution network may well be set up in order to enable other ships to follow suit, contributing to a zero-emissions shipping industry, but not yet a zero-emissions hydrogen manufacturing process.

Liquid hydrogen is not produced on a sufficiently large scale in Europe, although a Norwegian refinery looks set to at least begin to alter that situation. This is positive thinking, even if the manufacturing process is still very dirty. But cargo carriers, bulk carriers, and even oil tankers need to follow suit, pretty damn quick, and I suppose that's a remote possibility. What is *not* possible is that the people in India or Pakistan, or in cities such as Nairobi or Kinshasa (unless they are very rich) will be driving a hydrogen fuel cell car anytime soon – and I strongly suspect that only the financially buoyant will be doing so here in Wales, too. This still leaves a significant and un-closable energy gap. If, by the universal nature of simple bad luck, you happen to live in that gap – *you are in big trouble.*

Such vehicles, aircraft and sea transport might *just* be available to the few by the time the oil runs out (or becomes no longer viable), but travel by them will not be cheap. Neither will public transport, and the bicycle will find a new lease of life in a much slower, much more localised way of life.

But before then, when oil is still the principal energy source of the world and the price has skyrocketed, life will be hell. Homes in the winter will be freeze boxes, their owners forced to build chimneys and burn coal. Public transport will run intermittently on anything it can get its hands on or maybe, in the countryside, not at all. Holidays will be a past dream, a memory caught on an aging smart phone, and second-hand TVs and computers will quadruple from their original shop price. In the summer we all either bake to a crisp or drown.

I see no way around any of this, unless Dieter Helm is right and there is enough oil to fry the planet several times over. If so, we have to leave most of it in the ground, unless we wish to contemplate the end-times through the miasmic smell of burning flesh. Either way, we need to act *now* to procure a variety of forms of non-oil, non-gas, energy sources. Not next year, or the year after, or the year after that – but *now!*

Fifty to seventy-five years *after* the oil has gone (let us hope it's that short) and the gas with it, things will be almost back to normal, at least in terms of transport. Trains will run, and maybe even on time. Cars will be affordable again. Planes and ships will be running on hydrogen fuel cells as if the oil had never existed; some of them may still be electrically sail-operated motor sailors, carrying as much cargo as they do now.

However, all this is determined by how and when they solve the dirty manufacturing problem and can obtain entirely free, clean hydrogen. Until then, life will not be back to normal. Global warming will continue to worsen. If clean hydrogen can be recovered, *enmasse*, either from water or the atmosphere, it will eventually seem as if oil, gas, and coal never existed. But that's ninety to a hundred years or more, from now. Unfortunately, that's not what your kids and mine will experience.

CHAPTER 4

"We must face the prospect of changing our basic ways of living. This change will either be made on our own initiative in a planned way, or forced upon us with chaos and suffering by the inexorable laws of nature."

James Earl Carter, 39th President of the United States

Saudi Arabia is the source of most of the world's oil. It is a huge country, larger than Yemen, Oman, Syria, Jordan and the United Arab Republics put together. It is larger than Iran and was once almost entirely composed of desert. For centuries the area had been ruled by the Rashid clan along with the remnants of the Ottoman Empire. In 1902 Abdul Aziz, the self- elected king of Arabia, captured Riyadh after a fierce battle and expelled the Rashid dynasty.

Aziz then proceeded to cross large parts of the Arabian Peninsula, conducting successful battles against various towns and villages, until eventually he proclaimed himself the King of Hadja, Sultan of Najid, and by these means controlled most of the area now known as Saudi Arabia. In this far-reaching conquest he was supported and encouraged by the strictest and most zealous Islamic sect in history: the Ikhwan, a group that might be described as the ultra-conservative right within the already fanatical Wahhabi sect.

Just as President Kennedy, closely assisted by his father, used the Mafia to gain power and then attempted to annihilate them (instead, along with the possible aid of the CIA, they annihilated him), Abdul Aziz turned on the Wahhabi. He fought them for four years, before finally bringing them into his sphere of influence. This sect has not disappeared, however, and to this day plays a role in the strict religious control over the population of Saudi Arabia. After thirty years of almost constant conflict, the brave warrior that was Abdul Aziz, on 22 September 1932, declared his realm of sand dunes as far as the eye could see as the Kingdom of Saudi Arabia.

He ruled for twenty-one years over a poverty-stricken and little-known kingdom, his only source of revenue being the fees he charged to pilgrims making their way to Mecca. But as the wind-blown sand dunes move from place to place in Saudi Arabia, the world itself was moving. And although the world may not have heard of Abdul Aziz, he had heard of the world. He was well aware of the rise of Nazism in Germany and the fact that Zionist immigrants were beginning to escape from Europe and Nazi domination by purchasing land in Palestine. And he did not like it. Not one little bit.

To say that Abdul Aziz was a naïve sand Arab, who understood little except how to put up a tent, would be a gross insult. He was very aware that if the Jews established any kind of a foothold back in Palestine, the security of the entire Middle East region would be destabilised. And he made every effort to alter that possibility.

He also understood power and how it worked. Business opportunity seemed to be in his blood. He arranged for the first oil explorations to be conducted, which led to some remarkable possibilities, but all based on the understanding that when, and if, oil was discovered it belonged to the Saudis. Not to anyone else. And although a 50/50 agreement was the best that could be achieved in 1950 with the oil company Aramco, by 1980 Saudi

Aramco was formed and finally controlled all the Saudi oil.

However, by as early as 1982, the spin had begun. Detailed, field-by-field information about reserves and production was restricted, and Saudi Aramco began reporting to the Organisation of the Petroleum Exporting Countries (OPEC) that its proven reserves amounted to 170 billion barrels. This was sixty billion barrels more than a previous figure quoted by Aramco, but close to the figure reported to the United States Senate. So, the question arose: where did these fresh oil reserves come from? Had the Saudis increased their reported reserves, by adding probable reserves to proven reserves?

In 1988 to 1989, the figure jumped again to 260 billion barrels although no new fields had been found – not one. This figure was considerably higher than previous figures but curiously close to the 248 billion first reported in 1970. Reserve growth, also known as 'field appreciation', are the names given to finds of more oil than expected in the same well. This does happen. In fact, the current increase in world production over that of several years ago is caused by just that phenomenon. But that makes the oil demise worse, not better, because very few new fields are being discovered, causing the ones we have to be scraped dry as you read this text.

*

In 1937, the King of Saudi Arabia, Abdul Aziz, conducted a series of talks with the deputy to Major General Sir Percy Cox (Colonial Administrator to the Middle East) and Lt Col Dickson, who also later became administrator to the Middle East. From the conversations it was obvious that the Saudi's millennium-long hatred of the Zionists had not dissipated in the slightest. The Arabs truly hated the Jews with an intensity that was biblical, leading to the king urging the British government to maintain Palestine under British sovereignty *forever* if necessary, and not to partition it into an Arab and a Jewish state.

In 1945 the king met Roosevelt and Churchill on the heavy cruiser warship, USS Quincy, on the Great Bitter Lake in Egypt. At this meeting the two leaders promised to give Saudi Arabia military aid in perpetuity, in exchange for oil. That agreement still stands. Following a further meeting in Alexandria with Churchill and Roosevelt, the ship steered for home. During these meetings King Abdul Aziz continued to voice his extreme displeasure at the possibility of a Jewish homeland in Arabia.

On 25 April 1945, King Aziz sent one of his favourite sons, Prince Faisal, to the first meeting of the then forty-five nations of the United Nations. He was to point out that President Roosevelt, before he died, had indicated that a Jewish homeland would not be made available to the Jews in Palestine, but maybe could be arranged somewhere else, such as in Africa. His appeal was completely ignored and Faisal returned, nurturing a deep dislike of the United States government, which did not stick to its promises from one president to the next. This was unknown in Saudi Arabia's all-powerful desert kingdom, but certainly not unknown to the indigenous American Indians, or the rest of the world for that matter.

Twenty-five years later, during the 1973 Yom Kippur War, when Prince Faisal had become King Faisal and America, the UK, and other European countries were obviously supporting Israel in the war against the Arabs, he got his own back (as he always said he would) and would not supply a single bucket of oil. This caused the very first US oil crisis. The oil embargo included not only the US and the UK but also Canada, Japan, the Netherlands, and later Portugal, Rhodesia, and South Africa. Queues at petrol stations, particularly in the US, were miles long and fist fights, even gun shots, became the norm.

King Abdul Aziz died in 1953. He was succeeded by his two sons, Saud and Faisal. This not unnaturally led to a power struggle, with Saud becoming the new king and Faisal the crown prince. By the time of the king's death in 1953, the astonishing early finds (which they absolutely did not expect) had become virtually 840,000 barrels per day out of five huge oilfields.

The two brothers were like chalk and cheese, with Saud being the cheese. He absolutely loved the opulent life style he had inherited, with his huge palace, Rolls Royce and Lamborghini cars. Faisal was the chalk: a religious zealot, pious, sober, academic, and something of a financial wizard.

His brother Saud set about spending at a rate equivalent to a miner's widow who has just won the lottery and then, by sheer luck, won it again. The country suffered. In fact, it teetered on the edge of bankruptcy, even though millions of dollars were pouring into the coffers. True, he had inherited a $200 million debt from his father, which, by simply ignoring it, had soared in 1958 to some $700 million, enough in 1958 to buy a small country outright.

In the early 1960s Saud travelled abroad, and while he was absent Faisal instigated a coup d'état, forming a new cabinet and therefore control of the country. Four years later Saud returned and threatened to mobilise the Royal Guard against his brother. The threat never transpired and Saud agreed to abdicate the throne to Faisal (for a very large sum, no doubt). Saud bin Abdulaziz Al Saud, died in Athens, Greece, in 1969.

Faisal bin Abdulaziz Al Saud, was not at all like his brother and the alarming debt was soon paid off by diligence, frugality, and commonsense. Plus, by now, oil revenue was pouring into Saudi Arabia like water over Niagara Falls. A month after taking the crown Faisal appointed his half-brother Khalid to be the new crown prince, while another half-brother became the Minister of Defence.

As a king, Faisal is credited with rescuing the country's finances and implementing a policy of modernisation and considerable reform. His main foreign policy themes were pan-Islamism, anti-Communism and pro-Palestinian nationalism. He successfully stabilised the kingdom's bureaucracy, and his reign had significant popularity among the Saudi population. In 1975 he was brutally assassinated by his nephew, Faisal bin Musaid.

From 1966 until his return to Saudi Arabia, Faisal bin Musaid, the king's assassin, was educated in America. He was not considered particularly bright, although he did eventually manage to obtain a bachelor's degree in political science from the University of Colorado. He had also studied English at San Francisco State College and briefly attended the University of California at Berkley. In 1969 he was arrested for selling LSD and given a year's probation.

On his return home he began teaching at Riyadh University. On the 25 March 1975, he went to a meeting known as a Majlis, in which the ruler listens to the requests of petitioners. He joined a Kuwaiti delegation and lined up to meet the king. The king recognised his nephew and bent his head so that his nephew might honour him in the traditional Arabic manner; Faisal fumbled a revolver out of his robes and shot his uncle twice through the head. He fired a third shot that missed completely.

Guards with drawn swords forced him to the ground and arrested Faisal bin Musaid, while the king was immediately rushed to hospital where he died from his wounds. Before he died, he managed to convey that he did not want his nephew executed. The Majlis was being televised and the TV crew captured the entire assassination on live television.

Nevertheless, whatever the dead king wanted, a Sharia court found Faisal bin Musaid guilty of murder in the first degree, and he was publicly beheaded in a square in Riyadh with a single stroke of a gold-handled sword. Immediately following the execution his head was displayed for fifteen minutes on a pointed wooden spike.

The Arab media implied that the execution of the king was a CIA-planned assassination, which seems highly unlikely. It was also rumoured that Faisal had told his mother of his intentions. She told King Faisal that her son intended to assassinate him, and he is supposed to have replied that, "If it's Allah's will, it will be so." Apparently, it was Allah's will–but it may have really occurred, not because Allah thought it was a good idea, but because King Faisal prohibited his nephew from leaving the country in view of his excessive drinking and drug consumption abroad. His nephew had also been bitterly complaining that his $3,500 a month (in 1975) was insufficient to live on.

The king was replaced by his father's next oldest son Khalid, who reigned from 1975 to 1982. He was a successful ruler, an honest and open man who got on well with the American president Jimmy Carter. He did much to bring peace and harmony among the tribal chiefs and religious authorities. He was also the de facto prime minister of the Saudis and concerned himself with the healthcare, education, and infra-structure of the country. During his reign the building of entire cities took place, while the oil flowed as if there was no tomorrow and it would never, ever, run out. He died from a heart attack at the age of sixty-nine in 1982.

He was replaced by yet another brother, Fahd bin Al Saud, who suffered a debilitating stroke in 1995. Fahd could not continue as regent, so his half-brother Abdullah took over his duties; he later became monarch on Fahd's death in 2005.

Abdullah was recognised as the king of Saudi Arabia and custodian of the Two Holy Mosques. He had once been mayor of Mecca. He was a close friend to the UK and the USA, purchasing billions of dollars of defence equipment from both countries; he also gave women the right to vote for municipal councils and to compete in the Olympics. He married thirty times and had more than thirty-five children. He was the third wealthiest head of state in the world, with a personal fortune of $18 billion. He died at ninety in 2015, in a country altered from a desert of sand as far as the eye could see, to a beautiful land of skyscrapers and contoured buildings, an experience to behold – a shopaholic's paradise full of squares, parks and greenery – but still, little short of a gulag to Saudi women, and a veritable slave camp to African and Philippine domestics, who are often so terribly abused they commit suicide.

He was succeeded by the present king, his half-brother, Salman bin Abdulaziz Al Saud, who has finally granted women the right to drive after July 2018, and the right to attend football matches (as long as accompanied by a male escort in all cases).He has also made negative comments about Muslim extremism.

The day-to-day running of Saudi Arabia has now passed to his son, Crown Prince Mohammad bin Salman, who has publicly declared that he will cut off the fingers of any journalist or critic of the royal family. He appears to have not just cut off the fingers of a relatively modest journalistic critic, but ordered him cut up alive, partly thrown down a well and dissolved in acid.

*

Saudi Arabia might be still be repressive, anti-feminine, anti-Jewish and vehemently anti-Shiite, anti-black, anti-alcohol, and have the unenviable reputation of treating servants and foreign workers like contaminated vermin. But it's still a hell of a place to look at, and a hell of a place to be in the oil industry – *for now!*

The repression in Saudi Arabia does not *apparently* emanate directly from the current king, who has to step as carefully in his own country as a hod-carrier walking amongst day-old chicks. The problem is quite simply Wahhabism, founded by Muhammad ibn Abd al-Wahhab (1703 – 1792). It is an ultra-conservative form of Islam that has, in the past, found a way to live alongside the House of Saud and is the 'force majeure' from which all the above antis emanate.

This fundamentalist viewpoint, this ultra-conservative attitude, exists in many Saudi groups and so-called charities, and has existed in certain representatives of the House of Saud too (believe me, they don't escape scot free). These charities have unquestionably supplied arms and money to what they call freedom fighters. However, in close scrutiny, they appear to be anyone, or any group, who is anti-Iran, anti-Shiite and, finally, anti-Christian: hence anti-Western.

The majority of mainstream Muslims, not just in Saudi Arabia but world-wide, strongly disagree with the interpretation of Wahhabism and many denounce them as a vile sect. Islamic scholars, including those from the Al-Azhar University in Cairo, the premier establishment of Sunni intellectualism in the world, regularly denounce Wahhabism as a satanic cult.

Wahhabism has been accused numerous times, and not just by the West, as being one of the direct principal sources of global terrorism. It has inspired the ideology of the Islamic State of Iraq and the Levant (ISIL), and caused disunity in Muslim communities by labelling entirely normal Muslims who disagreed with the Wahhabi definition as apostates, therefore justifying their being killed. It has also been roundly criticised for the destruction of historic shrines, of saints, mausoleums, and other Muslim and non-Muslim buildings and artefacts.

Similar sources of income, which may not be directly associated with the current King, Salman bin Abdulaziz al-Saud, or his son Prince Mohammed bin Salman, but nevertheless are theoretically accountable to the king, have financed and built 120 new mosques in Bosnia Herzegovina since 1990, and many new extreme, right-wing Muslim schools. Islamic radicalisation in the area has been noted by German newspapers as an extremely dangerous trend which is known about, but has been suppressed by the German government.

Wahhabism, which first developed in the eighteenth century in Saudi Arabia, is identified by the European Union as the main source of global terrorism. To be fair, the Grand Mufti of Saudi

Arabia, (the religious and legal authority in Arabia) has condemned ISIL and ISIS and all the other extreme Jihadist movements in the past, in the strongest terms. He has said, "The ideas of extremism, radicalism and terrorism do not belong to Islam in any way."

This is quite a comment, considering the Grand Mufti is a direct descendent of the founder of Wahhabism. But he has also said that Iranians are not Muslims: to which, of course, the Iranians take extreme umbrage. (Saudi Arabia is likely to instigate a war with Iran soon – *you heard it here first.*) The problem is that other members of the House of Saud look more kindly on the movement, applauding its staunch opposition to Shi'ism, its Salafi piety, and its adherence to the original secretive Ikhwan practices of Islam.

The current king, as well as the Grand Mufti, has also made it clear that extremism will not be tolerated, and that Wahhabism will be reined in, in future. For which outspoken comment, I suspect his personal security has just been trebled.

*

But watch this magnificent space when the oil runs out. Watch these beautiful buildings and expensive villas when there is no viable occupation and no viable alternative to that occupation – and then watch the above Ikhwan-type bedlamites re-emerge from the woodwork. You cannot pump hydrogen out of the ground for free, and the technology that was required to build places like modern Saudi Arabia out of the desert sands was, and is, entirely based on oil. The same situation will never come again – never! – In the entire history of the world.

There is no magic wand; there are no alternatives to this late, industrial age, supersonic lifestyle. Certainly a few mega-rich individuals, particularly in the Saud dynasty, will have their vehicles converted to run off hydrogen (one way or another) and the air-conditioning systems in the palaces will probably also run on hydrogen – at great expense, of course.

Saudi Arabia is the OPEC leader and its royal family, along with its Gulf allies, have spent the past few decades investing their oil profits in massive sovereign wealth funds, prepped for a rainy day in the desert. Certain reporters have qualified that these states will be able to exploit multiple trillions of dollars, currently held in huge bank balances, to keep body and soul together as they spearhead an internal economic revolution without oil.

Nevertheless, no country has the finances to air-condition and hydrogenise an entire nation, and currently the Saudi power stations run off gas turbines or oil. They have no nuclear power stations. Out in the desert the oil wells will fall into disrepair the pipelines will rust away to nothing, and large parts of Saudi Arabia will once again look like Mars.

The tribulations that will affect the vast majority of people will be catastrophic, particularly when their air conditioning doesn't work anymore, and their cars are pulled by mules or they learn to use a skateboard. They will also fry in the super-heated climate conditions – which are almost upon us.

Today, as I write this chapter, another daughter of mine, who is a nurse in the Australian outback, has phoned to say she is experiencing temperatures close to 49 degrees Celsius. If it wasn't for the air-conditioning units running full-pelt on electricity generated by oil or gas, or maybe coal, all the patients would die.

Across Australia's New South Wales, eighty-seven bush fires have blazed. It was so hot, dairy cattle dropped dead in the fields. And on January 15, 2019, a million dead fish, cooked while still alive, lined the banks of the Darling and Murray rivers. Through heat evaporation both rivers became shallow and extremely hot.

January 2017 was recorded as the hottest so far in Sydney, at

47 degrees Celsius, while Pakistan experienced over 50 degrees and Iran saw the temperature soar to 54 degrees Celsius. Human physiology is not designed to cope with the temperatures predicted for large swaths of the globe and many parts will soon become uninhabitable.

In the US, extreme heat caused more fatalities between 1978 and 2003 than earthquakes, hurricanes, floods and tornadoes combined. In France, the 2003 heat wave killed nearly fifteen thousand people, and during June (2018) massive peat fires could be seen from space blazing a path across the moors of northern England (*New Scientist*, 20 January 2018, p37). Meanwhile, in California, seventy-nine people are now recorded to have died and 700 still missing from 7,579 separate wildfires that have destroyed hundreds of homes over an area of 1.7 million acres (*New Scientist*, 24 November 2018, p6).

Huge stretches of the Middle East will soon be unliveable and the occupants will have to move or die. Strangely enough, aside from the Poles, Africa might be the place to be, because I suspect most people will go back to their tribal urban lifestyle, which had (and still has) little reliance on oil. In central Australia (if the heat continues) without air-conditioning most people will die. Even in Sydney, if things continue, a lot of people will die, particularly the elderly. In fact, everywhere where it is now already extremely hot, and if there is no future means of continuing to operate air-conditioning systems cheaply, people will die in the thousands.

*

The importance of oil and gas cannot be exaggerated. Without them countries will dissolve piecemeal, like the ice in an abandoned martini. Currently six or more Chinese cargo ships have violated the United Nations sanctions against North Korea by delivering oil, according to a Wall Street Journal report. Photographs taken by a satellite controlled by the American security services show Chinese-owned or operated oil tankers headed for North Korean ports, thus contradicting claims by Beijing that the nation had stayed true to its commitments under the new sanctions' agreement.

The ships involved were identified by the names still on their sterns. China had previously committed itself to halt the normal fuel shipments as part of an international effort to pressure North Korea into forfeiting its nuclear weapons and long-range missiles programme (which it still hasn't). After entering port, the ships probably made a secretive ship-to-ship transfer of the oil. American evidence also shows the ships making every effort to disguise their activities. Apparently, the vessels purposely turned off their automatic identification systems (AIS).

This is, strictly speaking, an illegal act and clearly dangerous, as demonstrated by the recent collision of an Iranian and Chinese tanker in the East China Sea. Both vessels, for unknown reasons, had disconnected their tracking systems at the time of the impact. Ships can be seen on radar, if they are in range, but it's impossible to detect a ship's name, cargo, or destination, unless the AIS are operational.

United States sanctions against North Korea have concentrated on oil but China has traditionally and perennially been wary of cutting off North Korea's oil. After the latest missile test by North Korea, the US intensified its pressure on Beijing. Among the options that were once being considered was to destroy the missile launch sites before a launch is possible, destroy the weapons stockpiles, or sweet-talk them out of possession. Although, surprisingly, a treaty was recently attempted in which Kim Jong-un of North Korea, instigated an apparent 180-degree turn around, and has told the US it will dispense with testing or even possessing nuclear weapons – we are, of course, still awaiting the results, and I suspect we will wait forever.

In the interim, China's main oil field, Diyang, is costing China $750 million in losses every six months. While the other field, known as Shengli, cost over $1.4 billion last year alone: both markedly unprofitable enterprises. China is currently at a loss as to what do about it. Chinese oil, and its available tight oil, peaked this year (2018).

China's tight oil situation is badly constrained by water issues. These forthcoming problems are huge and will undermine China's continuous growth and challenge any kind of sustainable society. In short, China will revert to massive coal use (which already accounts for 66 percent of its energy use) and which is anyway also destined to peak in 2020. They will have to import the last of the available oil at an extortionate price. Or go to war. The South China Sea has reserves that are yet untapped (they are not massive and will only last a few years) but China will claim them, and so will the USA. Watch this space because it won't be pretty.

CHAPTER 5

"When faced with a terrifying prospect, a common human response is to shut one's eyes. The loss of civilization and the resulting vulnerability most of us would experience is a frightening prospect that provokes an instinctive desire to become short-sighted, if not completely blind."

Stephen Leeb, *The Coming Economic Collapse*

You may never have heard of Stephen Leeb. Before I started researching the coming oil catastrophe, I certainly never had. But I now know that he is one of the many experts in the mining and oil industry who are trying to open peoples' eyes to a coming disaster: a disaster about which everyone is unquestionably myopic.

Since 2007 Stephen Leeb has been head of the advisory board of Leor Exploration and Production. Since 2007 he has also been a member of the advisory boards of Electrum USA Limited, and Sunshine Silver Mines, in Kellogg, Idaho, one of the world's most successful silver mines. These are companies that explore for natural resources, especially precious metals and energy sources, such as oil. He is also a member of the board of The PlainSight Group, an innovation company centred at Yale University. In other words, he is no slouch. He knows what he is talking about.

Leeb recently predicted the Dow Jones rise above 14000 and the collapse of the dot.com bubble. Leeb has (in the past) accurately predicted $100 a barrel for oil and the current bull market in precious and industrial metals. In *Defying the Market*, published in 1999, he also predicted the inadequacy of computers for solving the major challenges of the next and subsequent decades: in particular, the resource scarcity.

Leeb's most recent book, *Red Alert*, argues that the Chinese understand the issue of resource scarcity much better than the West. As a result of their accumulation of vital resources (even though the extraction cost is extortionist) they may leave the West in a nearly untenable position within the next decade.

There are many people like Stephen Leeb, tucked away inside the energy and mining industries, who can see all too clearly that we are on the threshold of a coming disaster (whatever Dieter Helm has to say on the subject). They write books, and they are well-written academic type books, but only academics seem to read them. You probably haven't, and I freely admit that until recently, I hadn't read even one.

I don't expect, for example, you have read Richard Heinberg's *The Party's Over*, or James Kunstler's *The Long Emergency*, or Matthew Simmons' *Twilight in the Desert*. These gentlemen are also oil experts. Again, there are many like them, but who, amongst us ordinary folk, have read them? I would like it to be millions; as I'm sure they would, because they make it abundantly clear that we are sleepwalking into an absolute nightmare.

If a recent experience of mine is anything to go by, in which I took the opportunity to test out the available market, we all have a problem. A problem which these writers clearly point out is serious, yet is being ignored by just about everyone.

Fairly recently, in my home town in Wales, I was caught speeding by a police officer using a handheld device. They (the police) gave me the opportunity to pay a fine and receive three points on my licence or attend a course for several hours pointing out the dangers of speeding.

The course was not cheap at £95, but preferable to getting an endorsed licence. It was actually quite informative, professionally conducted, and the room was full of similar speedsters. Anyway, cutting to the chase, at one point questions and answers were being bandied around about hybrid cars. I took the opportunity to point out that recent predictions from experts in the oil industry have estimated that the world's oil will run out in thirty to forty years, (or less) with a marker placed around thirty five, and that there is no viable alternative on the horizon. And unless some form of hydrogen cell technology took off like a veritable rocket *right now*, we would not be driving down the single motorway of Wales. We would be skateboarding or riding bikes down the very centre of the damn thing.

Needless to say, you could hear a pin drop! Followed by guffaws of laughter, and the assertion that the oil will last for at least another hundred years: that windmills, solar panels and the new Swansea Bay tidal lagoon electric generating system (which has since been short-sightedly cancelled) will solve all the problems imaginable: that the possibility of running out of oil with nothing to replace it was absolute nonsense.

This was clearly the default view, and who's going to argue with a room full of fifty or more people? "Okay," I said. "But remember, you heard it here first – because you *will* hear it again."

And there lies the problem. The question of what happens when the oil and gas run out (or even the possibility that we may have to stop using them *before* they do actually run out) never arises in the minds of ordinary people. They remain certain that technology will fill the gap, like water running into and out of a sink with the same volume at the same time.

But it won't. It can't, even if peak oil is considered a conspiracy theory (which it patently is not). Even if there were sufficient supply to last a hundred years: *we can't use it for a hundred years, we can't use it for twenty. We have to stop now!*

Every expert questioned, every insider book of the industry read, makes it perfectly clear that, unless a miracle happens, there will be a large and disastrous energy gap. If by chance you happen to be living in that gap, life is going to be desperate, and possibly very short.

Even if that scenario does not, for whatever reason, play out in the manner forecast by oil experts, we still have to stop. *So, the result will be exactly the same as if the oil and gas had run out,* and there will *still* be no energy source of any international value to replace them.

Oil academics and freelance oil geologists (the ones not mouthing the various oil companies' spin) know this: know this for sure, and are very worried. They are writing books about it, even though being a writer is not their profession and entails a great deal of work.

The truth is, the British general public (and one suspects the European and of course the American public) would rather watch game shows, soaps on TV, or cat videos on YouTube, than think about very much at all (as occurred at the fall of Rome). Pathetically ignorant of the facts and assuming that the serendipitous period history has dumped them into will last forever, they stumble blindly along, assuming every technical problem will be solved (by somebody else of course), while nursing the unspoken belief that fossil fuels and the lifestyles won from this energy source are endless. So, they couldn't care less.

The Ukrainians (and a few other ex-Soviet satellites) know better.

In January 2006 the Russian gas company Gazprom, because of disputes over prices and debts, with the Ukrainian company Naftohaz Ukrayiny, cut off all supplies of gas to the Ukraine, because the pro-Western, European-oriented country, would not, or could not, pay the price Putin and the company were asking. So, the Ukrainian company diverted some of the gas intended for Europe to its own domestic use. The pipeline in question is huge in both length and dimension. It originates in the desolate Arctic region of Bovanenkovo, on the Yamal Peninsula, 4,300 kilometres away from the nearest European end users.

The pipeline passes directly through the Ukraine. When the Russians discovered what was happening, they threw a fit and cut off the pipeline in midwinter for four days. It was 32 degrees Celsius *below* freezing. Other countries once allied to the Soviet Union have also had their gas cut off for varying periods of time, including Belarus, Georgia, and Poland. This pipeline is what brings gas to Europe.

The situation became calmer until 2007, when new disputes began over Ukrainian gas debts. In 2008 this led to a further reduction of gas supplies. During the last months of 2008 relations again became strained when the Ukraine and Russia could not agree on the debts owed by the Ukrainians.

By January 2009 disagreements had caused supply disruptions in many European countries, with eighteen separate European countries reporting either major reductions or complete cut-offs in their gas supplies from Russia. By September 2009, both Russia and the Ukraine stated that they felt the situation was resolved and that there would be no more conflicts over gas.

However, in October 2009, the disagreement with Ukraine began again, this time, concerning the amount of gas the Ukraine would import in 2010. The Ukraine intended, as a result of its reduced industry needs, brought about by an economic recession, to import less gas in 2010. Gazprom was not at all happy about that possibility, insisting that the Ukraine fulfil its contractual obligations and purchase the previously agreed quantities of gas, whether they wanted to or not, whether they needed it or not.

In June 2010, a Stockholm court of arbitration ruled that Naftohaz must return 430 billion cubic feet of gas to a Swiss-based company 50 percent owned by Gazprom because the Ukrainian company had deliberately stolen and diverted gas from pipelines passing through the Ukraine in 2009.The Ukrainian government was forced to admit that this was indeed the case, but stated that the return would not be quick.

In 2018, Russia declared that it will no longer supply Europe via the Ukraine, but will instead divert the pipeline past the Ukraine. Russia has already substantially reduced the volume of gas it transits across Ukraine.

In view of the sadly worsening relations between Russia and the UK (close Russian flybys and nuclear annihilation threats, plus the previous assassinations of Alexander Litvinenko and Gareth Williams of GCHQ Cheltenham, including the poisonings of Sergei and Yulia Skripal, leading to the expulsion of Russian diplomats from numerous European countries), it might finally be politic to start fracking here too, whatever the protests and the temporary environmental outcome: even though all fracking does is delay the inevitable, and of course it's also extremely dangerous. But since we depend to a large extent on Russian gas (about 20 to 30 percent), now might be a good time to start.

*

The dangers of fracking are legendary and not to be overlooked. During a twelve-year span in Colorado, a worker has died on average every three months: victims of an American system less concerned with workers safety than a turnover of $15 billion, in an industry which receives less scrutiny from safety inspectors than does a roofer or an ordinary house builder. According to the Bureau of Labour Statistics 1,333 workers died in the US oil and gas fields from 2003 to 2014 (*Denver Post,* 25 September, 2016).

Although actual fracking (splitting rock with high pressure

water, sand and chemicals) is theoretically not allowed in UK National Parks, a system of dissolving rock with acid is not banned in such parks and will shortly be used in the UK. In fact, the energy company Cuadrilla Resources has jumped the gun and is already using conventional hydraulic fracturing in Little Frampton in Lancashire.

*

To some extent the default view – that all will eventually be okay, held by so many people – is understandable, because, in part, they have not been told the truth, and in part, they *don't want to hear the truth*. Most people cannot entertain the possibility that civilisation teeters on a slender ledge; such thinking seems unnatural and abnormal. How could a civilisation that invented or discovered almost every damn thing on the planet possibly lose control of itself at the last minute and plunge into a sort of eighteenth-century existence for fifty years or possibly longer?

It's incomprehensible to them. They could, quite reliably, point to thousands of past British achievements, such as the six mentioned below, quite at random, and say: 'It's not possible that stepping back into a culture 150 or 200 and more years in the past, could happen to us. Some developing nation somewhere, maybe – but certainly not us!'

1930: The Plessey Company in England began manufacturing the Baird television receiver: the first television receiver sold to the public.

1930s: Radar was pioneered at Bawdsey Manor by Scotsman Robert Watson-Watt (1892–1973) and Englishman Henry Tizard (1885–1939).

1931: Stereophonic sound, more commonly known as 'stereo' was invented at EMI in Hayes, Middlesex, by Alan Blumlein (1903–1942).

1933: The 405-line television system, the first fully electronic television system used in regular broadcasting, was developed at EMI in Hayes, Middlesex; also by Alan Blumlein under the supervision of Sir Isaac Shoenberg.

1936: The world's very first regular public broadcasts of high definition television began from Alexandra Palace, North London by the BBC Television Service.

1964: Use of fibre optics in telecommunications was pioneered by Englishman George Hockham (1938–2013).

We are a bright nation, and industrially and technically led the world for well over a hundred years, while Russia, China, and Japan remained unknown, unacknowledged, backwater serfdoms. But Putin, as head of the GRU assassins in the UK, has so succinctly pointed out, we are no longer the British Empire, and we no longer rule the world. Nevertheless, how could Britain possibly allow itself to fall into the trap of not having any kind of replacement for oil or gas?

Well of course, we know that we do have a replacement, once we have sorted out how to extract hydrogen from a clean renewable source. In the meantime, we may have to replace the oil with dirty hydrogen, but at least we would then have a viable energy source – dirty or not. We could presumably worry about a cleaner system later.

But again, the same old question arises: will the water start running out of the sink faster than it's running in? Will there be an energy gap? Every expert I have spoken too – every single one: says YES! And some think the energy gap will cover decades.

The International Energy Agency (IEA), in a new report, has said that global carbon dioxide will keep rising, particularly in India and China where energy demand will double in twenty years. The IEA expects global demand for oil will lead to shortages as close as the 2020s (*New Scientist,* 17 November, 2018, p7).

The Department of Energy has said, 'Reforming low-cost natural gas can provide hydrogen for fuel cell electric vehicles as well as other applications – today'. However, the department then adds '*Over the much longer term,* the department expects that hydrogen production from natural gas will be augmented with production from renewable sources, such as nuclear and coal (with carbon capture and storage).The pressurised carbon could even be used to flush out the remains of the oil, and subsequently stored in the depleted oil-wells.'

Note – *over the much longer term!* And note the possible use of coal (carbon capture or not). Coal currently produces over fourteen billion tons of carbon dioxide annually. The most promising future technology using coal involves using the coal to make hydrogen from water, then burying the resultant carbon dioxide by-product.

The problem, as ever, is that so much of the terminology incorporates spin. The so-called 'clean coal revolution' is being used to describe super-critical coal-fired plants without carbon capture, on the basis that they produce less CO_2 and are running at 42 to 48 percent thermal efficiency. These are usually described as high-efficiency, low-emission (HELE) plants. In Japan, China, and South Korea, 70 percent of coal-fired energy comes from these super-critical and ultra-super-critical generating stations: hence, continuing to contribute to global warming.

The idea behind 'carbon capture' is actually very simple. You retain the CO_2 produced while burning the coal in the power station, compress it, pipe it under pressure away from the power plant to somewhere safe, such as deep underground, where it can be trapped and capped beneath impermeable layers of rock to prevent it from coming back to the surface or seabed.

Most European countries are considering (note considering) this option to reduce CO_2 emissions since it will allow them to continue using coal to provide electricity to maintain economic growth and living standards. The problem of course, is that such a scenario would normally include very long pipelines in many – if not most – cases and therefore be vulnerable to breakage or damage, by tectonic-plate movement, earthquakes, severe flooding, terrorists, or similar disasters. It is also eye-wateringly expensive. So, guess what is likely to actually happen!

The Kyoto Protocol was an attempt to reduce emissions even as energy needs increased worldwide. The original protocol emerged from a United Nations summit. 'The Summit in Brazil' in 1992 was a valiant attempt to prevent dangerous anthropogenic disturbances within the climate system. The USA declined to become a member; consequently, the protocol (so far) hasn't worked worth a damn.

There may yet be another unique, long-term answer, according to Henry Fountain of the *New York Times,* 26 April, 2018. A type of rock exists throughout the world but is principally in situ in large quantities in Ibra, Oman. It might become the saving grace

of the world – in that it eats CO^2 and turns it into more rock.

Ibra, Oman, is a very remote and desolate area of the Arabian Peninsula that sees the occasional goat or camel, but is otherwise a long way from anywhere. In Ibra, there exists a rugged set of sharp, rocky outcrops, which amazingly react with carbon dioxide and turn it into stone. Even the spring water that bubbles out of the rocks in places becomes infused with carbon dioxide and produces a crust of carbonate on the surface that looks similar to ice.

The process is called mineralisation, and could theoretically be harnessed and used extensively on a huge scale to soak up some of the billions of tons of CO_2 in the atmosphere. Capturing CO_2 may become an essential part of reducing climate change and since such rock formations also exist in other places, using it becomes a possibility. But how one actually goes about doing so is not entirely clear. It has been suggested it could be broken down and spread around the entire world's coastlines.

Roger Aines, who leads the development of carbon management technologies at Lawrence Livermore National Laboratory, in California, has said, "It's clear that we're going to have to remove carbon dioxide from the atmosphere, and we're going to have to do it on a gigaton scale."

*

Hydrogen fuel cell vehicle emissions are, we know, lower than emissions from gasoline-powered internal combustion engine vehicles. The only product from the tailpipe is water vapour. But even with the upstream process of producing hydrogen from natural gas, as well as delivering and storing it for future use, total greenhouse gas emissions are cut in half, and petroleum use is reduced by over 90 percent compared to today's gasoline vehicles... The problem is – at the expense of repeating myself fifty times – that neither the renewable system, nor the dirty system, can possibly duplicate all the various dependencies on oil in time to stop worldwide chaos. It simply cannot, even if, and when, CO_2 is made into artificial petrol, a fuel which has already used up its carbon and would therefore (theoretically) be carbon neutral (*New Scientist*, 17 March, 2018, p34).

The distant future will undoubtedly throw up some clever ideas and products which are being considered (and occasionally manufactured) even now, by a few specialist companies. But they are few, and struggling hard to be heard.

One example, as proposed by Carbon 8 Aggregates (UK), is using carbon dioxide directly from industrial emissions or somehow stripping the gas out of the atmosphere to make a building material similar to concrete using industrial waste and contaminated soil. Meanwhile CarbonCure, Canada, is also making a stronger and greener concrete out of carbon dioxide, while Solida Technologies, in New Jersey, USA is making a concrete out of CO_2 that needs less water and uses less manufacturing energy.

Covestro AG in Leverkusen, Germany is manufacturing polyurethane mattress foam from carbon dioxide. Using the gas as a fertiliser is another contemporary method that is being experimented with. Even a synthetic fuel called Blue Crude will soon be manufactured in Germany by Sunfire GmbH, in partnership with Audi. In America, Oberon Fuels, in partnership with Volvo, Ford, and Mack the truck manufacturer, are currently making a synthetic diesel from carbon dioxide that emits less particle pollution, and no sulphur.

Even more astonishingly, Mayi Arcellano Panlilio, et al., at the University of Calgary, in Canada, has genetically engineered the bacterium *Escherichia coli,* to change human faeces into a 3D printable plastic named polyhydroxybutyrate. Small tools (or should I say 'small stools') such as spanners and mole-grips have already been made from this plastic which functions like any other hard plastic. The material is biodegradable (*New Scientist,* 14 April, 2018, p15).

These wonderful ideas and start-up companies will one day inspire sufficient other companies to use the excess CO_2 in our atmosphere and the excess human waste in our sewers for a hundred different purposes.

But that day has yet to arrive. And right now we are a very long way off.

*

There is no doubt that the winding down of oil and gas supplies will necessitate huge price rises. This in turn will push up food prices, making it impossible for minimum wage earners and difficult for even medium wage earners to survive, and even more difficult to get to work, unless that work is close enough to reach by bicycle.

Graham Turner, of the Melbourne Sustainable Society Institute, has pointed out that the concept of peak oil seemed to have been refuted, as fracking in the US produced a surplus that sharply reduced oil prices. But rising prices, in the very week in which I write this sentence, indicate this bonanza is already close to an end. Hundreds of oil geologists and oil experts know this, and they have predicted the social and economic result. Some of the predictions are truly catastrophic. If (for example) a weatherman told you it was going to rain all next week – knowing, as you do, that modern weather reporting is pretty accurate – you would be inclined to believe him.

If these geologists could get their message out as clearly as the weatherman they certainly would, and you would believe them. They are, after all, experts in their field. But the subject is fraught with politics, irresolvable engineering and technical problems and more secrecy than SIS (MI6) (the British Security Agency that spawned the fictional James Bond). So their message is diffused and seemingly apparent only to those educated in energy resources, and those retired from the oil business. Or it is simply ignored.

CHAPTER 6

"Let me tell you something that we Israelis have against Moses. He took us forty years through the desert in order to bring us to the one spot in the Middle East that has no gas or oil."

Golda Meir, fourth Prime Minister of Israel

But Golda Meir was wrong: Moses didn't do such a bad job after all. Gas was discovered in Israel in 2009, and there are some strong Israeli views on the subject – if nowhere else than in the Nuclear Engineering Department of the Ben-Gurion University.

In 2010, a year after the discovery, Professor Arie Dubi of the Nuclear Engineering Department, gave an interview during a lecture. It's now 2019 and the situation has not improved. It's become much worse.

The lecture began,

> "For some time now flames have been seen shooting up from one of the drilling sites of Givot Olam Oil Exploration. Givot Olam investors have been spotted nearby celebrating. There is plenty of excitement over the new gas discoveries in Israel, which are said to be a genuine treasure for the nation, worth hundreds of billions of shekels. But not even these new gas discoveries, can save us from the troubles to come in another fifty years."

Professor Arie Dubi is a sixty-five-year-old academic at the Nuclear Engineering Department of Ben-Gurion University, in Israel. He is a tutor, a lecturer, and has a PhD in physics. He once founded a start-up company to develop a programme predicting 'systems behaviour' using the mathematics of nuclear physics. He has published three scientific books; one has been translated into Chinese. He has always been outspoken about the coming oil and gas problem and has made his opinions clear in numerous lectures concerning the oil apocalypse.

He has been reported as saying,

> "Fossil fuel energy sources, coal, oil and gas, are running out. All the researchers in the field have known this for a long time. I'm not a prophet, this is a real situation. It doesn't matter what Yam Tethys finds, or what the Delek Group the controlling shareholder of Yitzhak Tshuva discover. It's insignificant on the global level. This type of energy will be gone within fifty to a hundred years. Just because it's in Israel means nothing. It's meaningless. Israel must continue for a long time. We're talking about the future of our children and grandchildren. Oil energy is running out, and that's it, there won't be any more. We're already witnessing that to extract oil its necessary to go five kilometres offshore like British Petroleum. If there were enough oil, they wouldn't be drilling in the middle of the ocean, which is very difficult and we can see the results."

The professor has spoken much more openly in conversations, interviews and lectures, than other academics about his concerns for the successive generations in Israel and elsewhere.

> "We must think ahead. A world without oil is a world without food, and that means a world war, in which billions of people will die. I do not see a different reality. Will we go back to eating bananas off the trees? No. Wars will

> break out; people will take the little fuel remaining and fight over it. You don't need to be a genius to understand this. After all, what do people do in times of want? They go and take what's there."

An interviewer asked the professor about the possibilities of solar energy.

> "Anyone hanging their hope on that might as well hang themselves as well. I have nothing against wind and solar energy, they're great and we need them. But all the alternative energy sources, such as solar, wind and wave all put together can't even supply forty percent of what we need."

The professor made it quite clear that the answer is nuclear power. He was then asked, 'What exactly *is* nuclear power?' He replied,

> "Atoms are surrounded by electrons containing energy that we recognize as a chemical-like fire-and there is also energy *inside* the atom, which is released when neutrons hit the nucleus of the atom and split it. This fission produces energy. The mass of the results of fission is smaller than the original mass; the difference in mass turns heat into energy. Atomic energy alone can supply one-hundred percent of the world's needs."

He was again asked, 'If we have already discovered the ultimate solution, what's stopping us?'

> "Terrible ignorance, mostly; there is a myth of fear surrounding nuclear energy. Our first encounter with it was at Hiroshima and Nagasaki. The first time people were aware of nuclear energy they saw four hundred thousand deaths. But this is only one side of this energy. It's like the difference between fire in a kitchen gas range and a hand grenade: Both produce chemical energy, but the gas at home helps us. We don't fear it or worry that it will explode. It's hard to explain this to people."

This Israeli professor is absolutely right of course. We need all the renewable energies, but the backbone, the mainstay of electrical generation, must be nuclear. It's a technology we understand and already have. Currently France leads the way with nuclear energy, and it is right to do so. The professor continued.

"The problem is not just Hiroshima and Nagasaki. On April 26, 1986, Chernobyl in the Ukraine exploded. The explosion contributed greatly to people's fears about nuclear energy and although apparently caused by a combination of human error compounded by lax safety precautions during an experimental run, leading to a partial meltdown of the core, and a massive never previously witnessed release of nuclear radiation, amounting to thirty times more radioactive fallout than the two Japanese bombs combined. Causing everyone to now believe that such an energy source is extremely dangerous – *but it isn't*! Fukushima in Japan has since added to the fear by being ridiculously close to an ocean that had historically seen tsunamis before. None of these manmade or natural accidents negate the efficiency, or indeed the need for nuclear power stations. Countries that have overcome this fear have been successfully producing electricity from nuclear energy for years. France is the most prominent example, with 80 percent of its electricity supplied by nuclear reactors. France's entire economy is based on nuclear power and it supplies electricity to all of Europe. If France turns off the main switch, northern Italy wouldn't have electricity."

France is of course, not alone. Nuclear plants provide electricity in the United States, Europe, and Asia, and new reactors are being built in many countries around the world: Slovakia is currently building four new reactors, Slovenia one, South Africa two, the Czech Republic three, and South Korea twenty-four. Nuclear power currently operates in thirty-one countries.

China has thirty-eight under construction. The UK currently operates nine nuclear power stations and the Japanese company Hitachi is (or was) building two new ones, one on Anglesey and one in Gloucestershire (production is now on stop because of escalating building costs and lack of British government financial input. Greenpeace, naively think this is excellent news – but of course it isn't).

The interviewer then asked why Israel has no nuclear power stations at all.

> "That's a tough question. Let's start with the fact that nothing is done in Israel. Have we solved our water shortage? If it's possible to do nothing, we do nothing. Why? It's political. And politicians live best when they do nothing. When they do something there's complaints and shouting. Ehud Olmert went to war and almost got killed over it. Had he done nothing, maybe he would have been okay. In Israel, first of all, nothing is done. Then there's the security problem. People are afraid even when there's no reason. Someone once asked me, 'is a nuclear reactor strong enough to resist an atomic bomb?' And I said, 'someone's throwing an atomic bomb at you, and you're worried about the reactor?' It just goes to show the level of stupidity and fear."

The professor continued,

> "There are three types of reactors in the world today, a giant one-thousand to three-thousand-megawatt capacity; but a small ten-megawatt reactor buried in the backyard could provide electricity to the average home for forty years. The Americans and the Chinese use these. The third is a medium-size, two-hundred-megawatt reactor that can supply power to an entire region, such as the Negev and the Arava Desert. The latter type could also be coupled with a water desalination plant. Just imagine a canal from the Red Sea to the Dead Sea, in which water is

desalinated – we could turn the Arava into an oasis."

The professor went on to suggest that Israel could even build and sell such reactors. He was asked, 'How much would they cost to develop?'

> "There are still no exact figures because we're not there yet. But let's say we had to invest twenty billion dollars in the project: so what? If a reactor sells for a billion and you can sell 20,000 of them, doesn't that pay?"

He was then asked how easy it would be to get such approval in Israel for that kind of spending, 'Wouldn't it be very difficult?' asked the questioner.

> "True, but we don't have to do it alone. We can cooperate with other countries. Many countries want to get into this field. It's an opportunity to develop something that would solve our electricity and energy problems for the future, provide jobs to a thousand engineers and earn a lot of money for the state."

The interviewer commented that the United States and Israel appear to be in perennial fear of other countries in the Middle East that do have nuclear energy or a reactor, but *apparently* have no intention of attempting to make an atomic bomb: Iran in particular. He was asked whether it was possible to make such a bomb using a civilian reactor.

He replied,

> "No! Even if it were theoretically possible to create enriched nuclear material like plutonium in a civilian reactor, it's so difficult and complicated that there's no cause for concern. Even if you take the best scientists in the world, and they try to do it together, they won't succeed. The enrichment being carried out by the Iranians, for example, is a million times easier. Nuclear fuel is enriched to between 4 percent and 12 percent, but nuclear

explosive material requires 99 percent, enrichment. No one will ever be able to remove fuel from a nuclear power plant and use it to make an atomic bomb. *It's entirely paranoid nonsense.*"

The interviewer asked whether, in the future, there was a real economic chance that a nuclear plant could be built in Israel.

> "I've discussed this with many people, including the National Infrastructure Minister Uzi Landau. The ministry's Chief Scientist's Office issued a report saying that within thirty years, Israel will require such a reactor. That is, they believe we must start to act in twenty-five years. But one of our biggest problems is that the government is oriented toward the private market. It wants to privatize whatever it can; including reactors. But, as I told the chief scientist, privatizing reactors is like replacing the army on the northern border with a private security company. It's about as logical. An important matter like energy cannot be left to private hands, where the only consideration will be profit. Perhaps a reactor won't be as profitable as they would like, but it will give life."

The professor continued,

> "The danger is not only the lack of fuel, but also population growth. People have no idea of the disaster that awaits us. In 1950 the global population was two and a quarter billion. Now sixty years later, there are six and a quarter billion people. In historical terms between the time of the first human beings and cavemen to the first half of the 20th century, it took us thousands of years to reach two and a quarter billion, and just another half century later the figure has nearly tripled. In another fifty years there will be thirteen billion people." (*The New Scientist journal estimates humanity will need Two Earths to support itself by 2030*)

*

This was an unusually long discourse. However, the concerns voiced by this Israeli professor are real. They need to be heard, and listened to, because they have to be faced. Lack of energy and population overgrowth is a lethal combination. Within the period of the Industrial Revolution a huge change took place. Whereas it had taken all of previous human history, until around 1800, for world population to reach a single billion, the second billion was achieved in only 130 years (1930). The third billion in thirty years (1960), the fourth billion in fifteen years (1974), and the fifth billion in only thirteen years (1987).

During the twentieth century alone, the world's population has grown from just over one and a half billion to six billion. There are currently, 2019, almost eight billion people in the world. By 2020, there will nine billion. The consequences of such a population boom will make Israeli attempts to bribe the African immigrant refugees to go back home, and the labour migrants who have crossed the Egyptian border into Israel illegally, plus the refugees piled up in Europe and on the Mexican border, look like a joke. When there is no oil and no food and no means of obtaining instant energy, what do you think is going to happen to all these people?

Eight years ago, the professor said,

> "Millions will be migrating, looking for food. At the same time there will be an energy problem as the population keeps growing. There will be a big war, billions will die and the world will start over."

*

And it's not just Israel that's facing problems.

Scottish academics from the University of Edinburgh, led by Professor Roy Thompson, of the School of Geosciences, have recently completed an in-depth study of the oil and gas reserves available to the UK in the North Sea. The findings are that only 11 percent of oil remains and 9 percent of gas and at present rates of consumption these will run out in *ten years* or less.

The Edinburgh University scientists also stated that hydraulic fracturing, known as fracking in the popular press, will be barely economical, especially in Scotland, because of geological complications. In fact, Scotland has just refused to re-allow fracking (its first attempt was stopped in 1961) after a consultation found overwhelming public opposition and little economic justification for the industry. Paul Wheelhouse, the Scottish energy minister, told ministers of the Scottish Parliament that allowing fracking would undermine the government's ambitions to deeply cut Scotland's climate emissions, and would lead to unjustifiable environmental damage.

Professor Thompson has said, "The UK urgently needs a bold energy transition plan, instead of trusting to dwindling fossil fuel reserves and possible fracking."

Hydraulic fracturing is the correct terminology for obtaining oil from shale rock by injecting large quantities of water containing additives, including sand and lubricating fluids, into it. Shale gas, or oil, is confined *inside* the impermeable shale rock. This differs from the conventional deposits under the North Sea that are confined under pressure below impermeable rock which has to be drilled straight through to obtain the gas.

Simply drilling into the shale in much the same way will not work: the rock has to be cracked open, fractured at a sufficiently high pressure to get the gas or oil out. Hydraulic fracturing techniques have been used in the UK for some years, even in conventional deposits, but mainly offshore. Now the UK government is allowing attempts to extract gas and oil from the shale rock onshore, in an attempt to increase the UK's production of fossil fuel energy.

The technology of fracking is not, strictly speaking, complicated, but it is unquestionably messy, and involves drilling down vertically some two kilometres and then laterally outwards one to three kilometres. The gap between the lining of the borehole and the surrounding rock is then sealed with waterproof concrete or a steel tube. The well casing is perforated to allow fluid to get into the rock, and gas to get out. On the average well, up to ten million litres of water containing sand, lubricating fluids, and chemical additives are pumped into the borehole at up to 9000 lbs per square inch pressure. This opens up 50-metre cracks in the shale. When the pressure is released the cracks are kept open by the sand particles, enabling the shale gas to escape. A well head is then installed to capture the released gas and the drilling equipment moved to another site.

Clearly there can be as much energy used to obtain this result in the first place, as is eventually obtained from the well in the second place, but the government remains undaunted and is convinced this will reduce our reliance on imports (particularly from Russia) and generate economic benefits. The largest expanse of shale rock is situated in the countryside, between Lancashire, Yorkshire and Lincolnshire. This is where the majority of economically viable sites are likely to end up.

So far, only the company Cuadrilla Resources has started to drill using conventional hydraulic fracturing in the UK shale deposits, although licences have been issued for the rock dissolving technique (rather than the direct rock fracturing technique). It is not yet known how much gas or oil will be commercially recoverable, but the current estimate is in the region of 1,300tn cubic feet.

In America the technique has developed rapidly over the past ten years, and now has 1.7 million oil, gas, and fracking-type wells throughout the United States. Hydraulic fracturing, if handled incorrectly can be a serious environmental hazard, and the US has shown us how *not to do it*. The robustness of the safeguards through regulation in the United Kingdom is critical, if environmental and human harm is to be prevented.

*

One of the biggest problems is: what happens to the discarded water full of chemicals? It's usually pumped into a nearby containment lake, which you definitely can't swim in, and which tends to infiltrate the local groundwater and nearby rivers. The volume of water used is mind-blowing and automatically lowers the available water table. For example: it takes almost *two million* gallons of water to complete each fracturing operation, plus 40,000 gallons of chemicals comprised of 600 different types of additives, including some well-known carcinogens and toxins: like lead, uranium, mercury, ethylene glycol, radium, methanol, hydrochloric acid and formaldehyde.

There are more than one thousand documented cases of severe groundwater contamination due to hydraulic fracturing in the United States, and many cases of rivers being polluted. As previously noted, the British *were* apparently going to use the technique in which the limestone rock is melted or dissolved by acid. What happens to the acid afterwards is anybody's guess.

Acid rock drainage (ARD) or acid mine drainage is already a problem in mining, due to the acidic water that is created when sulphide minerals are exposed to air and water, a natural (not artificial) combination that accidently produces sulphuric acid. Acid rock drainage often (if not inevitably) introduces acidity and dissolved metals into the groundwater and nearby rivers, which can be extremely harmful to fish and other aquatic life.

Controlling natural ARD is an ongoing concern, both during all types of mining operations and after mine closure. Technology is gradually catching up with this problem, but hasn't resolved it yet.

CHAPTER 7

"It is evident that the fortunes of the world's human population for better or worse are inextricably interrelated with the use that is made of energy resources."

Marion King Hubbert, geophysicist and geologist 1903 – 1989

This is someone else you may never have heard of, but I can assure you everyone in the industry has. Every industry from fashion to mining has its gurus and proclaimed stars: sometimes well deserved, sometimes not. Hubbert was definitely an oil guru of note, who worked at the Shell research laboratory in Houston, Texas. During that time he made some very important contributions to geology, geophysics and petroleum geology. He is credited for the now famous (or infamous) Hubbert curve and the Hubbert peak theory. He was often referred to as King Hubbert.

In 2008 the price of oil soared to $147 a barrel and it was considered oil may have reached its peak (the point of no return). But it was not the peak, at least not the financial peak, and oil has recently jumped from $55 per barrel to around $70 per barrel and more recently still to almost $80 a barrel, but in 2019 has dropped again to around $55. In the UK it costs around $52.50 to produce one barrel which is trading at approximately $42. These kinds of ups and downs, including occasional very dramatic rises and equally sudden plunges, were all forecast by

King Hubbert a long time ago.

Hubbert was born into a poor Methodist community in hard-scrabble country (euphemism for poverty area) of San Baba, Texas; he sold a cow in order to go to college. He was sufficiently scientifically minded to understand very early on, how hydraulic fracturing might work, insisting that first drilling vertically then injecting fluid into the rock at great depth and at great pressure would spread the liquid horizontally, not vertically, as experts then believed must be the case. He insisted he was right, but of course they ignored him.

Later he attended the University of Chicago, achieving a Bachelor of Science degree in 1926, and his Master's degree in 1928, plus a PhD in 1937 in geology, mathematics, and physics. He taught geophysics at Columbia University and joined the Shell Oil Company in 1943, where he stayed for twenty-one years. On leaving in 1964 he became a senior research geophysicist for the US Geological Survey until he retired in 1976.

Hubbert is best known for his famous method of predicting, overtime, how much oil is left in the ground and therefore when it would peak. This included the study of oil field sizes and natural gas reserves and the limits these fields impose on the rate of oil and gas production.

Based on this theory he presented a paper at the 1956 American Petroleum Institute meeting in San Antonio, Texas, which stipulated that oil in the United States would peak between 1965 and 1970. His prediction received the same kind of reception as my comments at the speeding management course, simply because many other predictions by other people had eventually been found to be wrong.

In 1970 American oil production peaked and immediately began to decline, exactly as predicted by Hubbert. However, his forecast at the time, pitched him into a running battle with many bigwigs in the oil industry, until the oil crisis of 1973, when his prediction was proved to be correct. He thus achieved overnight oracle status during Jimmy Carter's term as President. This prediction, and others he got right, made him famous – at least in the oil and gas industry.

In 1974 Hubbert predicted that total world oil production would peak in 1995, but *only* if the then-current trends continued. Various subsequent predictions have been made by others as trends have fluctuated in the intervening years. The then-current trend did *not* continue, while in the meantime extraction expertise using water with partially hydrolysed polyacrylamide and xanthan, to drive the oil towards the well, became so much better that 1995 was passed at full bore without missing a beat.

He had nothing to say on the subject, just listening to the often-wrong predictions of others. He then finally forecast that global production of crude oil – oil found in pressurised reservoirs that flow freely up when wells are first installed – would peak around 2007 to 2010.

As mentioned earlier, crude oil peaked around 2006/2007, helping to pitch the global economy into recession. The International Energy Agency and most major oil companies agree that conventional crude production has indeed peaked. Hubbert's predictions made a lifetime before, were again proved accurate.

Although he was accurate in terms of conventional crude oil, he hadn't taken into consideration the unconventional sources, such as tar sands and shale oil. Although the crude had peaked, the difficult-to-get-at, tight stuff began to explode of the shelf (so to speak). Six million barrels a day was produced between 2006 and 2014. A fifth of this came from Canadian tar sands and the balance from the shale oil revolution which principally took place in the United States. Curiously, his overall prediction was skewered by the very production technique he had helped to develop sixty years before. (Currently 4.67 million barrels a day of crude oil is produced from tight oil: equal to 50 percent of the crude oil production of the entire United States.)

There are economists who would argue that this exposes the blind spot of Hubbert's approach. He never took into account the technology accessible to expand the oil resources we can extract and improve on. To point out that technology increases the amount available has been more than demonstrated. However, because it is tar sands and shale oil, which peak very early, it may not amount to more than a last gasp.

The future trajectory of tar sands and shale oil output is, strictly speaking, an unknown quantity. The Fort McMurray wildfire in Canada, which lasted fifteen months, covered 600,000 hectares, and cost over $9 billion Canadian, hasn't helped: having had, a large effect on the tight oil production situation in that country.

All experts agree fracking wells suffer vertiginous decline at rates of up to 50 percent in the first year. In the United States the high-yield places have already been tapped, and the industry is massively in debt. Furthermore, it is well known that even when oil was over a $100 a barrel it still wasn't possible to make an unsubsidised profit. The International Energy Agency, expects American shale production to peak in 2020.

If non-conventional production continues to meet growing global demand well into the future (which is considered very unlikely), the fame of King Hubbert and his famous bell curve prediction will fade into an historical footnote. That will also be the case if demand for all types of oil starts to decline sooner than the supply, due to improvements in efficiency and the hydrogenation and/or electrification of all types of vehicles.

The chances of this occurring have improved with the Paris climate agreement (even if the US stays out of it). Saudi Arabia also accepts such a scenario, having announced a $2 trillion fund to wean its own economy off oil by 2030. But what can possibly replace such a bonanza, such a freebee, such a remark-able gift from God, is difficult to imagine.

*

Besides all of the above, there are factors outside of the oil demise that give disturbing hints that Western civilisation is starting to crumble. As pointed out by the Paris based journal-ist, Laura Spinney, in the *New Scientist* journal January 2018 – *things definitely ain't what they used to be.*

She points out that creative interpretations of religious texts are not the only symbols or signs of a declining Western culture, and that it is reaching a critical juncture, as observed by scien-tists, historians, politicians and journalists who live in Llanelli as well as in Paris.

Cycles of inequality and resource are reaching a tipping point, she says, and I entirely agree. She is absolutely right. There are many examples of past civilisations coming to a point of col-lapse. But, as she correctly points out, who is looking? For the most part, she says, people are carrying on as usual: shopping or posing on social media. In fact – I would say – just about every-body seems blissfully unaware that such a collapse is only a short distance away.

She is basically saying what I am saying, and will continue to say in the following chapters. It is, however, nice to hear my favour-ite (and prestigious) magazine backing me up via a lady I have never met.

She also asks if science has any ideas about what is *really* happen-ing now and what will happen next? Is it possible to turn things around? She points out the glaring inadequacies in the Trump presidency, in that his ignoring international commitments are part of his electoral promise to 'Make America great again.'

She has said that,

"America looking inward, contemplating its own naval is

> a dangerous move that threatens to undermine the whole world order. Trump has even made things spectacularly worse during his July 2018 visit to Helsinki, in which he denigrated his own security service, apparently placing more trust in Vladimir Putin's opinions than his own advisers. *This is a president with less decorum than an alley cat.*" (My emphasis)

The consequence of America turning its back on Europe could be catastrophic, with that equally unpredictable brown bear in the East flexing its muscles and still sore from the collapse of its empire and subsequent loss of territory.

She is right, of course. The United States, and especially this current administration, needs to learn from other sources how to conduct itself with grace and still achieve prosperity. Unfortunately, the philosophical outlook of American business – in fact, Americans at large – is that you get ahead by being ahead, and you arrive there by being a bastard. The consequence is the wealthiest 20 percent in the United States are up to eighty-five times wealthier than the 80 percent balance of the American population. This is a simply staggering inequality of wealth, of which, most Americans are totally unaware (*New Scientist*, 31 March, 2018, p28).

Clearly there is something radically wrong with American capitalism as it stands at the moment. If it's true, that progress is based entirely on pushing others down to gain a foothold, rather than pushing up by innovation to gain an advantage (Bill Gates style), then the US is doomed. In Russia the situation between the 'haves' and 'have not's' is much worse, but hidden entirely from sight, as opposed to America (or even the UK), where it is hidden in plain sight.

Spinney has already been asked if science has any leads and if there is any evidence that Western culture is entering its end game. And she says that, according to Professor Peter Turchin, an evolutionary anthropologist at the University of Connecticut, there are certainly some worrying signs.

Apparently, the professor realised that the mathematics he was using to outline boom and bust cycles in animal populations could be used to describe the rise and fall of civilizations. So, in the 1990s he began to apply the same equations to historical data that link factors such as wealth, health, and inequality, to political stability.

Sure enough, he found pointers in all the collapsed civilisations of the past, such as in ancient Egypt, China, and Russia. He found that when the supply of labour outstrips demand, because of population increases, the wages drop and all labour becomes cheap (something we in the UK know all about).

Financial divisions become much more apparent, with a wealthy elite and a poorer, working underclass. As a society falls deeper into this trap, it enters a more destructive phase, in which misery of the very lowest economic strata, along with in-fighting among the elites (read politicians and moguls) contributes to social turbulence and eventually collapse *(see the current yellow jackets in France. It's just the beginning)*.

He suggests that this is followed by a second shorter cycle lasting fifty years, composed of two generations: one generation peaceful and the other turbulent (like Cain and Abel). He has discovered such anomalous peaks of unrest in 1870, 1920, and 1970, and predicts the end of the next fifty-year-cycle in 2020, in which case it will coincide with the turbulent part of the longer cycle. This will bring, he says, the kind of protests and social unrest seen during the protests against the Vietnam War.

Professor Safia Motesharrei, is another mathematician at the University of Maryland who has noticed that certain societies such as the Mayans, Minoans, and the Hittites, never recovered from their collapses because of extreme divisions between the 'haves' and the 'have not's', coupled with resource depletion. This type of coincidence can push a society onto the 'never recover again bench,' but only when the two problems – inequality *and* resource depletion – coincide. Because, he says, they fuel each other.

Inequality exists in abundance in the US and the UK, does it not? And I would suggest it exists just about everywhere else too. But let's face it: it's considerably more noticeable in the US than elsewhere, except perhaps Russia. So, we already have the first pointer – *inequality* – and the second one is racing down the outside lane at a startling pace – *resource depletion.* And we don't have to wait until the oil runs out. *Resource depletion* simply means serious shortages, and they will start to transpire, madam, before your pre-teenage son has had time to grow a decent moustache.

It's not a joke. Its damnably serious, and the professor says that part of the reason it will snap into place like a released elastic band, rather than creep up on us, is because the 'haves' are buffered by their wealth from the immediate effects of resource depletion and global warming for longer than the 'have not's', and so will resist calls for strategic change until it's too late.

That's exactly where we are now folks. And as Spinney points out, "That doesn't bode well for Western societies which are dangerously unequal as *overall* only one percent of the population owns half the wealth, and that division has been growing worse since the financial crisis of 2008."

The professor also points out that the West might already be living on borrowed time, and by rapidly depleting fossil fuels (non-renewable resources) a society will grow far beyond what its available resources could possibly support. But while the fossil fuels still flow, the TV soaps, the wine, and the whiskey flow too. When the collapse happens, she says – *and it will happen* – it will be so much deeper.

Such a scenario has happened before (on a minor scale) when, in 1849, the California gold rush brought thousands and thousands of the so-called forty-niners on the long hazardous journey to search for gold.

At first they found it, and everyone got along with everyone else just fine. Then, in a very short period of time, surface gold began to run out, and the miners who saw themselves as 'real' American citizens began to turn on the Chinese miners, the Mexican miners, the black and Indian miners, and, eventually, anyone doing better than they were.

In my opinion, American commercial violence and greed started there in 1849, and hasn't diminished since. Although, some academics I know think the real greed dates back to the Founding Fathers' acceptance of slavery as an economic necessity, hence, occasioning the need for paid slave patrols. This engendered a combination of greed combined with a lack of altruism – a caustic mix.

What is stomach churning, and so utterly disgusting that it's difficult to write about, is that over a third of the US Senate and House of Representatives, know this to be a fact. They are not, as they like to portray to the media, convinced by the climate change deniers who call themselves scientists. They know that the ice is melting, the sea is rising, the coral is dying, and the whole scene is human-made, or certainly human aggravated. They know it, but they take money from fossil fuel supported organisations, like Koch Industries and the Heartland Institute, to spout the opposite: to deliberately mislead the public: to obfuscate and deny and delay: to lie outright.

America has gradually become the world's Judas. It is going to screw the entire world over for money: fossil fuel money. Not *all* Americans, just those poisonous vipers that care nothing for the planet, nothing for the future, and nothing for their own grandchildren – *only money seems to motivate these people.*

CHAPTER 8

"Oil has made foreign and security policy for decades. Since the turn of this century it has provoked the division of the Middle East, aroused Germany and Japan to extend tentacles beyond their borders, caused the Arab oil embargo; Iran versus Iraq, and the Gulf war. This is all clear."

William Richardson, UK Secretary of Energy, 1999

The reason we need to change society *now*! – Not in the next fifty years, but now – is because the rot is already here: a rot which we all need to understand, and from which we must make every effort to recover. Everywhere and with everyone, there is a sense of dismay at social orders that are unfair and inaccurate. At groups that take advantage and consistently get away with it (such as that third of the US Senate receiving their thirty pieces of silver). At powerful men groping young (and not so young) women (in both the UK and the US) simply because they believe they hold all the cards. Of a remarkably unfettered, pouting, school-yard bully becoming president of the largest economy in the world, and the sad fact that many US citizens support him.

At government departments everywhere, that are grossly inefficient, making mistakes that Mickey Mouse could see coming, then try to squeeze out of their responsibilities. At utility providers; from electric and gas companies, to mobile phone and broadband suppliers, that woo you, then deliberately screw you.

Here are only a few of many such examples.

*

The car manufacturer Volkswagen deliberately misled the US in TV adverts and magazine articles, stating that their diesel cars were clean. And not just clean: squeaky clean. One advert even showed elderly ladies joshing each other about how diesel cars were either dirty or clean and proving the cleanliness by holding a white scarf tightly over the tailpipe. In the advert the scarf was unmarked. But the whole construct was subterfuge and obfuscation on a grand scale.

The cars were fitted with special software that recognised when they were being tested in a garage or a laboratory situation and controlled the nitrous oxide (N_2O) emissions so they always passed the garage emissions test. But when back on the road, the software switched the con-job off, ejecting forty to fifty times more than the legally approved amount of N_2O. On occasions, according to the University of West Virginia, eighty times more was being pumped into the surrounding air.

After months and months of denial, Volkswagen agreed to recall all the cars sold and correct the fault. They recalled them alright – only to upgrade or refit them with even more sophisticated software that made the fact that the cars were *still* emitting the same amount of noxious fumes even more difficult to discover.

Unbelievable and outrageous as it might sound, the above is perfectly true, and it took the combined efforts of various departments and specialists in the US to eventually get the car company to admit that what they were doing was deliberate, illegal, and a conspiracy to defraud. It was frankly outrageous and obvious that their sales and profits were more important than people's health and even lives.

To the chagrin of the prosecutors no one went to prison, although the company was ordered to pay $4.3 billion in fines and $15 billion in settlements. It was also made clear that all the top people in the company were aware of the scam and six top executives of VW were prosecuted for fraud. Not only was the company aware of what they were doing in the USA, they were, and are, fully aware of the fact that they are still doing exactly the same thing in mainland Europe *and* the UK where, to my knowledge, no protests at all have been raised, except convoluted methods of charging or restraining diesel cars passing through inner-city London.

And there you have it. A total lack of altruism: the core of the problem that lurks within the worst of capitalism and the worst of politicians. Such as the voluble climate denier Senator James Inhofe, the elderly archetypal Okie from Muskogee, who displays a *total lack of scientific understanding, allied to a similar lack of social integrity* – a circumstance that needs a constant jaundiced eye.

*

VW was eventually told to remove the deceiving software or they could no longer sell cars in the USA. They removed the software. The Americans had caught them cheating and did something serious about it. But in Europe, along with other European diesel car manufacturers, they do exactly the same thing, using the excuse that reducing the N_2O being ejected from the exhaust pipe damages the engine.

Never mind that it makes people seriously ill and damages human lungs, as long as it doesn't damage the engine (and their profit margins). After all, that's what matters? Despite the fact that ten thousand people a year experience a premature death due to diesel fumes in mainland Europe alone.

The UK government has already lost a series of court cases brought by Client Earth, because of its failure to take action to meet nitrogen dioxide limits. In early 2018 the EU said it would sue the UK and five other countries for failing to comply with EU limits.

*

The complications that surround all of us in this latter part of the Industrial Revolution are often times unbearable. We need to return to honesty, to integrity, to a simpler life. And although the post-oil world will hopefully bring these improvements it will also, initially, bring chaos and death on an alarming scale.

It's not just a question of depleting oil and the collapse of complex societies as an aftermath of that fact. It concerns the psychology of so-called democratic governments: the way they hide the facts from the electorate, the way they are never as transparent as they should or need to be.

For example (just one of many): the US government has misplaced, or misspent, with no indication of *where* it actually went...twenty-one trillion dollars. *Yes, you heard correctly* – $21 trillion. According to a report by the Reuters News Agency, the US federal government overspent $21 trillion between 1998 and 2015, with no account of where the money is, or where it went.

Mark Skidmore, a Professor of Economics at Michigan State University who is also a specialist in public finance, researched the documents of the Department of Defence and the Housing and Urban Development Department, as well as examining the reports of the Office of the Inspector General (OIG). He found, along with his team, that $21 trillion had gone completely missing. Furthermore, papers supporting the study also went missing, just as an audit was announced.

Professor Skidmore, on hearing that Catherine Austin Fitts, a former Assistant Secretary in the Housing and Urban Development Department in the George H.W. Bush administration, was aware that the Inspector General had found $6.5 trillion dollars for which the Department of Defence could not account, thought Fitts had made a mistake in the 26 July report, when referring to the missing money in *trillions*. She must have meant millions, or possibly billions. Based on his previous experience with public finances he thought the figure was too big, even for an organisation as large as the US military. He said,

> "Sometimes you have an adjustment just because you don't have adequate transactions, so an auditor would just recede. Usually it's just a small portion of authorized spending, maybe one percent at most. So, for the Army one percent would be $1.2 billion of transactions that you just can't account for."

But he soon discovered the figure was entirely accurate. After discovering that fact, he and Fitts collaborated with a pair of graduate students to comb through thousands of reports in the Office of the Inspector General, dating back to 1998, when new rules of public accountability for the federal government were set. They then brought the search forward to 2015, the year with the latest reports available at the time. Skidmore commented that,

> "This is as yet, incomplete, but we have found $21 trillion in adjustments over that period. The biggest chunk is for the Army. We were able to find thirteen of the seventeen years and we found about $11.5 trillion just for the Army."

The professor would not disclose, or even suggest, whether the missing trillions might have gone to some legitimate, but undisclosed, projects, was simply wasted, or was directly misappropriated. However, he believes his find indicates that there is something profoundly wrong with the budgeting process in the US federal government. He has said,

> "Such a lack of transparency goes against the due process of authorized federal spending through the US Congress."

This is clearly one markedly polite, if not slightly nervous, gentleman. The same week the Reuters interview took place, the Department of Defence announced that it would conduct the first-ever audit. Financial comptroller David Norquist told reporters that the Office of Inspector General had hired independent auditors to dig through the military finances. Skidmore commented that,

> "It is important that the Congress and the American people have confidence in the Department of Defence's management of every taxpayer dollar. While we can't know for sure, what role our efforts to compile original government documents and share them with the public have played, we believe it may have made a difference."

In early December 2017 the authors of the research discovered that the links to the key documents they had used, including the 2015 report, had been disabled. Days later the documents were reposted under an entirely different address.

*

It's not just car makers, pharmaceutical companies and government departments that spread the worldwide demise of honesty: banks have a great deal to answer for, too. Banks have consistently failed to keep promises. Banks have deliberately forced small business people to the wall. Banks have foreclosed on deals they themselves invented. Banks caused the housing market collapse in the United States and then profited. Banks launder dirty money.

Between 2010 and 2014 UK banks paid out the same amount in fines as they did in bonuses. Simon Rogerson of the user-friendly Octopus Group, has said,

> "How does an industry behave like that? When you have had to pay £38.5 billion in fines and compensation, how can you think it is right to pay yourself over £32 and a half *billion* in bonuses? It's no wonder this is the least trusted industry in the world."

And rightly so, because you would have to travel a long way to compete with the illegal activities of HSBC, the so-called Honkers and Shankers of the money laundering world.

2002: HSBC acquires Grupo Financiero Bital in Mexico although aware that the bank was highly suspect in terms of dirty money acquired from the drug cartels.

2006: Stephen Green, previously in charge of private banking, becomes HSBC chairman.

2007: HSBC realises the Anti Money Laundering Committee in Mexico is not functioning correctly, but does nothing about it.

2008: Hervé Falciani is arrested in Geneva. He had hacked into 30,000 accounts holding more than $100 billion in assets. He escaped to France where he was held but not extradited, especially when the authorities realised that the information he had included the names of thousands of tax evaders.

2010: Christine Lagarde, the finance minister in France prepares a list of names of people mentioned in the data taken by Mr Falciani for the use of other countries. It becomes known as the Lagarde list and results in arrests in the United States, Spain, Greece, Belgium and Argentina. In the United Kingdom, HMRC, Income Tax Department, obtains the details of a thousand tax evaders. Over £1035 million is recovered, but only one person prosecuted. No legal action is taken against HSBC.

2010: HSBC is investigated by US Senate investigators, who criticise the bank for providing Banco Africano de Investimentos, a private bank in Angola, access to the US financial system, despite João Lourenco's lax approach to the laundering of money through Angola's banks.

2010: Lord Stephen Green resigns from HSBC UK.

As a separate issue, a regulator at the US Office of Comptroller of the Currency observed problems in HSBC's own anti-money laundering practices. He therefore ordered the bank to hire a permanent regional compliance officer and submit full compliance plans in policing improper money flows. The compliance officer could clearly see fraudulent activity on his first day at the compliance office.

2012: HSBC is obliged to sign a five-year deferred prosecution agreement with United States prosecutors, after admitting that it was involved in accepting drug trafficking money and was also guilty of transmitting funds from Iran and other sanctioned countries. The DPA (Drug Policy Alliance) informs the bank that it will be prosecuted and lose its US banking licence if there are any further crimes in that period.

2014: HSBC, JP Morgan, and Crédit Agricole (the French bank) are charged by the European Commission for allegedly being involved in an alliance to manipulate the Euribor interest rate bench marker, as the three banks are standing firm against a settlement reached by the EC with other institutions. This case is ongoing.

2014: HSBC agrees that it misled people and mis-sold mortgage-backed securities and agrees to pay $550 million in settlement.

2014: HSBC pays US and UK regulators $618 million, as one of six banks fined a total of over $4 billion for their involvement in a foreign exchange rate rigging scandal.

From 2000 to 2010 HSBC laundered millions of Mexican drug cartel dollars through various accounts. HSBC was well aware of the fact and had derived various techniques to identify and hide the results. As one of the people interviewed by the Netflix programme Dirty Money said, "White people who live in big houses and drive nice cars and live in places like Connecticut get off – that's the reality."

In 2012, the same year that HSBC avoided prosecution, over nine thousand people were themselves prosecuted and went to prison for drug dealing offences. The bank was fined $1.9 billion. Not one single executive went to jail!

The Royal Bank of Scotland is another desperado that forced thousands of companies to the wall and asset stripped them with more expertise than a pole dancer: yet was found to have committed no crimes by the Financial Conduct Authority (FCA). Many victims and politicians are calling for a public enquiry. Several victims have committed suicide.

You think banking capitalism works? Oh it works alright – it works overtime.

*

The Vatican Bank is (or certainly was) the most unregulated bank in the world. It operates much like an offshore bank, only much more so. It is considered beyond reproach and therefore unapproachable and beyond the possibility of investigation by the Italian police. It is also massively corrupt.

At 7.30 am on Monday 18 June, 1982, the banker Robert Calvi was found hanging under Blackfriars Bridge in London. Calvi was chairman of the Banco Ambrosiano Seded di Roma, Rome's largest private bank. It collapsed in 1982, showing a £1.5 billion shortfall. Calvi was (among other things) being sought for illegally funnelling £30 million out of Italy.

Calvi had been surreptitiously laundering money for the Mafia for a long time (possibly with little choice, because one of the principal shareholders of the bank was the Mafia). But he was finding the problem of where to actually hide the vast sums involved difficult. That is, until he met the newly appointed head of the Vatican Bank, Archbishop Paul Marcinkus, an outgoing, boisterous Chicagoan that the Pope had recently promoted. The Vatican also had a 10 percent holding in the same bank and was well aware of the illegal transactions taking place at the Banco Ambrosiano.

Marcinkus knew nothing about banking, not a thing: but the pope liked his rough blustery personality and so he accepted the job and turned to Calvi to show him the ropes. This was a golden opportunity for Calvi to offload Mafia money where it could be safely laundered through the Vatican Bank. Millions, even billions, were laundered in this way, with the Vatican Bank receiving a percentage of the takings.

Calvi was a member of the illegal Masonic lodge 'Propaganda Due' frequented by the Mafia and popularly known as *Fratineri* or Blackfriars. The day before his body was found, Calvi was stripped of his post at Banco Ambrosiano by the Bank of Italy and his fifty-five-year-old private secretary, Graziella Corrocher, jumped to her death from a fifth-floor window at the bank's headquarters. Corrocher left an angry note highlighting the damage that Calvi had done to the bank and its employees. Corrocher's death was ruled a suicide by the British police.

The London police took a mere week to rule Calvi's death also a suicide. However, it was later proven by Mafia admittance (and by a private detective using much better forensic evidence than the police had even attempted to obtain) that the London-based Italian Mafia had killed Calvi for losing Mafia money during the problems associated with the bank. Weeks after Calvi's murder, his bank went belly-up, owing $1.5 billion.

Many believe that the death of Pope John Paul I, in 1978, just thirty-three days after his election, occurred because he wanted to break the shadowy links between what was then Italy's largest private bank and the Vatican. A year later, in 1979, the Italian journalist Mino Pecorelli, who had been investigating Archbishop Marcinkus, the Vatican Bank, and ties to the Mafia, was found murdered.

The mixed and complex dealings of the Vatican bank and Banco Ambrosiano's money laundering were worldwide and investigations in Italy continue to this day. The Vatican Bank, however, was deemed entirely innocent and no one from the Vatican was ever prosecuted, or even approached. Archbishop Marcinkus, who died at the age of eighty in 2006, was never even questioned.

*

In 2015, 11,500,000 documents were leaked to the German journalist Bastian Obermayer, who worked for the paper *Süddeutsche Zeitung,* by an unknown source calling himself John Doe. The leak concerned 214,000 offshore accounts belonging to the Panamanian law firm Mossack Fonseca. These accounts were of shell companies that existed on paper only: hundreds, even thousands of such companies shared the same address, usually an empty office, or simply a postal address. Such set-ups are neither unusual, nor are they necessarily illegal.

So much data was involved that the International Consortium of Investigative Journalists (ICIJ – of which I was once a member) became involved and 107 media organisations, in eighty separate countries, sorted through mountains of information.

Some of the owners of the various shell companies were surprising. The wife of the prime minister of Iceland, Sigmundu Daviö Gunn-laugsson: the prime minister of Pakistan: the king of Saudi Arabia: the Russian leader Vladimir Putin and his close associates: Syria's Bashar al Assad family: and David Cameron's father, who owned the Blairmore Investment Trust. Many countries' leaders were there, including well-known sports and show business personalities.

Most of these transactions might be considered morally debatable but were not strictly internationally illegal; they are simply a way of avoiding the country of origin's income tax demands or, in some cases, salting away ill-gotten gains.

However, among them, were dozens of companies on the original Forbes 500, including many top British, American, and European companies clearly avoiding paying tax to their respective countries, which is more than morally reprehensible: it affects us all. The less these discreditable companies pay, the more people in the lower income brackets have to pay. In America the loss amounts to $150 billion per year to offshore tax havens, in which the name of the real director (or directors) does not appear: a completely unknown name is automatically inserted.

But, more alarmingly, hidden in the voluminous amounts of paperwork were well known gangsters and narcotic traffickers, including the Mafia. Corrupt government officials and entire government departments. The DEA has said, "This method of hiding vast amounts of money is what keeps the cartels and sex traffickers alive."

If you are an American citizen you don't actually have to go offshore. In the US (which is now the third largest tax haven in the world) you can place your money in tax havens in Delaware, Wyoming and Nevada. In fact, thirteen states are considered tax havens. Delaware alone earns $1.2 billion per annum. Recently it was discovered that a Russian arms dealer named Victor Bout, who dealt arms to the Taliban, had loot in twelve shell companies in Florida, Delaware, and Texas. The rules applied to these American tax havens have since been upgraded and tightened somewhat: nevertheless, they are still tax havens where the singular idea is to avoid paying tax to the IRS.

In the UK we have Jersey, Guernsey, the Isle of Man, Gibraltar, Bermuda, British Virgin Islands, and the Cayman Islands. Sven Giegold, the European Green Party's spokesperson for economic affairs in the European Parliament has said that,

> "The British government has been hindering the European Union's fight against tax avoidance and money laundering for years, and we are particularly sceptical about the tax haven blacklist."

In April 2018, ministers finally announced plans to clamp down on a number of loopholes, including a notorious scam whereby criminals launder dirty money through the UK by means of a one-hundred-year-old idea called a Scottish Limited Partnership (SLP). These were first introduced in 1907 to financially aid farmers in Scotland but are now been being used by oversees criminal organisations, such as the Russian Mafia.

One such scheme, according to recent government research, used one hundred separate SLPs to launder $80 billion in corruptly obtained Russian money in only four years. Other East European criminal gangs (it has been discovered) used SLPs to move illegal arms around the world.

Meanwhile, according to Transparency International (TI), £4.5 billion worth of properties were purchased in the UK with criminal money. One in five is owned by Russians. The government says that it intends to put a stop to all these possibilities following the attempted assassination of Sergei Skripal and his daughter in Salisbury England, but financial journalists tell me the response so far is a profound zilch!

Supplying the fuel that keeps the Syrian jets flying comes from one of these kinds of sources, according to journalists from the Fusion Media Group of Miami Florida. The lack of international transparency on corrupt money laundering allows the most awful things to happen daily, from the sex trafficking of East European girls by East European thugs, to the barrel bombs dropped on Syria. The entire world needs a form of moral rearmament, but it might get it sooner than it expects when the oil runs out.

*

The American government (at least parts of it) can, on occasions, be vigilant in the prosecution of financial criminal activity, and we should all applaud that. Yet other parts of that same government, as described above regarding the missing $21 trillion, do not tell the truth about public finances, and have not been doing so for a very long time.

Who, for example, knew that the day before 9/11, Donald Rumsfeld announced that $2.3 trillion of government monies was unaccounted for (yet again) and had effectively gone missing? Meetings were taking place in an attempt to identify where the money had gone in the Pentagon office block into which Hani Hanjour flew American Airlines flight 77 – and on the very same day. The problem was never resolved.

Whether you want to call this worldwide gradual moral collapse of the social order, a slow-motion car crash, a progressive loss of complexity, or a form of social entropy (as do many academics, hiding behind fancy phrasing so as not to alarm the general public concerning the shocking lack of moral integrity sweeping the entire world) is up to you. Historian Ian Morris, of Stanford University in California, has simply said,

> "You have got to be very optimistic to think that the West's current difficulties are just a blip on the screen. *They are not.*"

CHAPTER 9

"We know it is impossible to go on finding, moving and wasting oil, levelling forests, paving land, dumping poisons, and multiplying our numbers. A new way of life, a new set of thoughts must be found."

Donnella Meadows, environmental scientist

Joseph Tainter, an anthropologist at Utah State University and author of the *Collapse of Complex Societies*, sees the worst-case scenario as an eventual rupture in fossil fuel availability, causing food and water supplies to fail and millions to die within a few weeks.

> "I foresee a pattern in the present leading to the future, where technological innovation is not going to be able to bail us out, as it has in the past. If the West makes it through, it will be more by luck than judgement. We are a species that muddles through, that's all we have ever done, and all we will ever do."

Muddling through might not do it. Aside from the failure of the current authorities everywhere to get to grips with rampant corruption, constant wars of attrition, and a worsening inability to control the Pandora's Box of cyberspace, all the pointers indicate that we simply cannot put up enough windmills, make enough hydrogen cell cars, planes, and ships in time. We simply don't have the resources; we don't have enough time left. But above all – we don't have the will…

Nevertheless, if we want to survive, we must find the money and the time: but above all we must find the integrity and the willpower for an entire planet - wide moral rearmament – and all at the same time.

*

The costs of supplying enough wind turbines in the US to eventually offset the demise of electric generating stations has been estimated to be $3,322.65 for every man woman and child currently alive on the entire planet.

In the UK, the population is already none too enamoured with the huge windmills that dot the countryside, and dotting is nowhere near sufficient. Even covering the entire island, until every citizen had a windmill in their back garden, would not come close to supplying sufficient energy for the UK's needs. Besides, have you any idea how much oil, steel, and current energy is used in the construction of a single wind turbine?

Without doubt, wind turbines have made huge differences to the economy and the lifestyle on some off-shore islands. On islands such as El Hierro in the Canaries, for example, wind turbines are the source of the island's *entire* electrical needs, plus having sufficient power to run a desalination plant. This clever idea not only supplies the islands drinking water but, acting as a battery-cum-reservoir, water is pumped up a mountain which then drives inline turbines as gravity drops it back down the mountain again. Hence it supplies electricity when the wind does not blow: expensive to build in the first place perhaps, but a clever use of entirely self-contained natural resources.

The beautiful touristic island of Madeira has accomplished something very similar. Wind turbines pump fresh water into a huge reservoir hidden inside a mountain. This then supplies electricity by using gravity to drop the water through massive pipes that enclose turbines back down the mountain to yet another reservoir, where it is eventually pumped back up again.

Not to be outdone, Orkney Island, in Scotland has now become the world's principal island for *blue* renewable energy (i.e., energy garnered from the sea). After first discovering offshore oil and becoming an oil tanker haven, it is now concentrating on wave energy based on concepts applied by the European Marine Energy Centre Ltd (EMEC), a UKAS-accredited test and research centre focusing on wave and tidal power. Many experiments on wave and tidal energy are being explored there. Blue power (as it is called) has a longway to go yet, but EMEC is certain it will one day supply the commercial energy machines of the future, because – unlike the wind – the waves and the tides never stop.

Wind turbines, are of course amongst the most visible symbol of the quest for renewable electricity generation, and we all know the wind is free. Nevertheless, the machines themselves and the subsequent structures built to maintain a continuous current flow are unadorned embodiments of fossil fuels.

Eight thousand separate parts have to be transported to the final installation point. Huge trucks are necessary to bring steel, concrete and other materials to the sites. Very large and cumbersome moving equipment is needed to access otherwise inaccessible high ground. Tall cranes are needed to erect the structures – and of course they all burn diesel at a rapid rate of knots. So do the freight trains and the cargo ships' that cross the countryside and the oceans to bring the assortment of materials needed for the production of cement and steel in the first place.

For a five-megawatt turbine 150 metric tons of reinforced concrete is needed for the foundations alone. The steel to make the rotary hubs and nacelles that incorporate the drive-train, the brake, the gearbox the generator and the control system amounts to 250 metric tons and 500 metric tons is necessary for the towers.

If, by 2030, wind-generated electricity supplied only 25 percent of the entire world's demand, which now amounts to something over thirty petawatt-hours (PWh), this would amount to 450 million metric tons of steel, having to be used to construct the turbines. And that's not taking into consideration the metal for the towers, wires, and transformers for the necessary high-voltage transmission links needed to connect to the worldwide grid. If again, by 2030, sufficient steel has been made to operate the thousands of wind turbines needed, a fossil fuels equivalent of more than 600 million metric tons of coal will have been used. Imagine how much carbon dioxide will have been thrust into the atmosphere during all of this.

A great deal of energy is used in making steel in the first place. Iron ore is first smelted in blast furnaces charged with coke and coal, plus infusions of powdered coal and natural gas. The pig iron is then decarbonised in oxygen furnaces until we eventually arrive at the famous puddler's poured molten steel, which is eventually turned into the final product. Steel used in turbine construction uses thirty-five gigajoules of energy per metric ton.

A five-megabyte turbine has three sixty-metre-long airfoils, each weighing approximately fifteen metric tons. They are made from Glass Reinforced Plastic (GRP) with epoxy resins and carbon fibres, and usually have foam cores. The GRP resins begin with ethylene derived from light hydrocarbons, the product of naphtha cracking, liquefied petroleum gas, or the ethane in natural gas. (There are now blades being made which are over eighty-three metres in length.)

After construction the entire structure must be waterproofed with epoxy paint whose synthesis also starts with ethylene. Another fossil fuel product is the lubricant for the turbine gearbox, which has to be renewed periodically during the machine's twenty-to-twenty-five-year lifetime. A well-placed wind turbine will theoretically pay back the energy used to build it in approximately one year. However, its initial production, installation, and maintenance remain critically dependent on fossil fuels.

It has been estimated that to get the required installed wind power by 2030 we would need an aggregate rotor mass of about 23 million metric tons, incorporating the equivalent of about 90 million metric tons of crude oil.

And, as already discussed, for almost all of these energies – coke for iron-ore smelting, coal and coke to fuel cement kilns, naphtha and natural gas for the synthesis of plastics and the making of epoxy, GRPs and carbon fibres, diesel for ships, trucks, and all the relevant construction machinery, lubricants for gearboxes etc, etc., – we have no substitutes that make sense, or that would be readily available on a requisite commercial scale.

Outside of islands with mountains, we need nuclear power stations. The very best available: not the cheapest, not the ones that make the largest shareholder profits, but the best and safest. And we need governments to build them, not private enterprise, not the Chinese, or anyone else, and we need them damn quick!

World electricity is not actually dependent on oil. Believe it or not, renewables compared to oil, in terms of generated electricity, are almost equal. See the graph below:

2012 World Electricity Generation by Fuels

▌Coal/Peat (40.4%)

▌Natural Gas (22.5%)

▌Hydro (16.2%)

▌Nuclear (10.9%)

▌Oil (5.0%)

▌Renewable (5.0%)

Although this graph was published in 2012, natural gas and coal, along with peat (which is equally non-renewable), still make up over 75 percent of fuels used to generate electricity in 2019.

In terms of generating electricity it's not the oil we have to worry about: it's the gas, coal, and peat. The gas will, of course, go first, followed by the peat and the coal; although the coal has a longer life ahead of it, it is still non-renewable. Were we to have the life of coal as a measure of time to come up with viable alternatives, we would probably manage to do so. Unfortunately, we do not have the life of coal, and coal will not fly planes, and it no longer propels ships.

So – no matter how you look at it, unless you live on one of the two islands above, you (or more specifically your kids) are looking at a bleak future, and it's the fault of the United Kingdom. It is, you know; it's our fault. We led you all into this industrial dream (or nightmare) which was never supposed to end, and was meant to continue from the spinning-jenny to the steam engine, to the moon and distant planets, and even the stars.

We didn't realise then, of course, what the end result would be. We always thought that, following the spinning-jenny, the more innovative the inventions, and the more of them that came along, the better. Maybe the Swing Riot farm labourers who destroyed early farm equipment in the UK in 1830 were right: maybe they had deep-seated instincts that crossed the centuries. Maybe the spinning-jenny, the machine that laid down the foundations for capitalism, made a wrong spin. Or maybe the wrong spin is not that old. Maybe the wrong spin was taken on 4 November 1980, when American voters, believing Republican propaganda, took the keys from Jimmy Carter (the hope of reason) and handed them over to Ronald Reagan.

But one day – one hopefully not *too* hot a day – far into the future, we will come out of this. We *will* start again, but not with fossil fuels, and not with corporate capitalism, and not with a Republican mentality. All three will be as dead as the dodo, deader than Beatlemania, gone and forgotten, in a world mostly running on sea power, wind power, and hydrogen, plus manmade fuels and lubricants and a form of political altruism and honesty that has no current name –since it will bear no relationship to any kind of historical '-ism'.

Or, we will experience a wasteland, a scorching hot desert in some parts and feet-thick in ice in others, with very few animals and very few people, all scrabbling to maintain a life somehow; anyhow. Let us hope it's the former.

*

Hope springs eternal – does it not? And some predictions are full of hope; humans will always be magnetically drawn to hope.

The Institute of Electrical and Electronic Engineers think that solar PV systems will end up being the most economical form of electricity within a decade. But only if the solar panel industry continues to improve solar cell efficiency and create real economies. James Prendergast, one of the company's directors has said,

> "As the cost of electricity from solar continues to decrease compared to traditional energy sources we will see tremendous market adoption, and I suspect it will be a growth limited only by supply. I fundamentally believe that solar PV will become one of the key elements of the solution to our near, and long-term energy challenges."

There is no need to wait a decade. As pointed out by the then research staff at Bloomberg New Energy Finance, in Finsbury Square, in London, in 2011. They saw solar power reaching grid parity (the point at which solar power is as cheap as the national grid) in the next two years. *Well, it's 2019 gentleman, and it certainly hasn't happened yet!*

In ultra-sunny regions like the Middle East, the researchers contend that solar power is already competitive. In fact, Saudi Arabia (which is right in the sun-belt) intends to build huge solar facilities in the near future. Coal currently costs approximately seven cents a watt, compared to twenty-two cents for solar. These costs will soon be equal: but what of our gas glut? Won't there be a natural instinct to use it? Will that not slow solar development in the future? The Saudi Arabian government says it will not: and they intend to build huge solar complexes to rival anywhere in the world. Meanwhile, the US has placed tariffs on solar panel imports in a bid to boost its own manufacturing sales. The result was markedly reduced overall consumer sales.

Reuters has clearly stated that, in their opinion (no matter how altruistic the intentions), natural gas produced from shale will kill the economics of renewable energy in the coming years. This is what they had to say:

> "As solar and wind prices continue to fall, natural gas will stay on top. Because even if, say, offshore wind costs the same as natural gas by 2015 (as predicted by German utility EON), there is still the extra cost of building backup power for when the wind doesn't blow. As long as prices are cheap, it's simply easier for utilities to opt for 'always-on' fossil fuels, instead of intermittent renewable sources."

How right can a news agency be?

The International Energy Agency believes that renewable energy will grow from 8 percent of total energy use in 2009, to 13 percent in 2035. But conversely, coal and natural gas will also grow. Energy generation from coal will increase by 25 percent from 2009 to 2035, and shale gas production will grow nearly fourfold during that same time frame.

So much for cutting down on carbon emissions.

A research team from the Stanford Research Institute, in Menlo Park, California, believes that by 2050 *we could* power the planet entirely with renewable energy: that is, if we ensure, by law, that all new energy production plants use renewable energy by 2030 and convert existing plants by 2050.

In this enthusiastic prediction, 90 percent of energy production would come from wind and solar and the other 10 percent would come from hydroelectric, geothermal, wave and tidal power. As Stanford has clearly pointed out we COULD power the planet entirely from renewable sources. The problem is not *if* we could. The problem is – *will we?*

Cars, trains, ships, and other forms of transportation would use hydrogen-powered fuel cells, and aircraft would run on hydrogen fuel or artificial fuel made from CO_2. The only problem they foresee is how to effectively beat back the fossil fuel industry to a point of non-existence. This is the pipe dream we have previously been despairing of, but one that we should at least aspire to. Check back in 2050, assuming you don't have to resurface in a nuclear submarine (in the manner of a disaster film) from a boiling sea to observe a blistering wasteland.

*

There are people and organisations (usually related or allied to the oil business, in one way or another) who think peak oil can be dismissed as a serious argument.

The following is from an OXREP (Oxford Review of Economic Policy), assessment by Professor Dieter Helm at Oxford University and Fellow of New College Oxford. He is an economist specialising in utilities, infrastructure regulation and the environment.

January 2016. Professor Dieter Helm.

> "Peak oil can be dismissed as a serious argument. The combination of the shale revolution and the ending of the commodity super cycle probably point to a period of low prices for some time to come. This is unfortunate timing for current decarbonisation policies, many of which are predicated on precisely the opposite happening – high and rising prices, rendering current renewables economic.

Low oil prices, cheap coal, and falling gas prices, and their impacts on driving down wholesale electricity prices, are the new baseline against which to consider policy interventions.

The confounding of expectations has an historical parallel. At the end of the 1970s, it was assumed that oil prices would go ever upwards, and the power of OPEC would grow. The US under Carter's presidency opted initially for solar and nuclear. Carter even had solar panels installed on the White House roof.

Europe decided nuclear was the answer. France pushed through its massive nuclear programme (at one stage building six nuclear power stations simultaneously), and Britain announced in 1981 that it would build ten new PWRs – one per year – Germany, Italy, Switzerland and Belgium followed suit. Japan, like France, aimed for over fifty reactors. Canada added another ten. Most countries boosted indigenous coal too.

All of this was based upon the widespread belief at the end of the 1970s that the 1980s and 1990s would see a further doubling of oil prices. When this failed to materialise, the great hopes for nuclear and solar fell away, exacerbated in the US by the Three Mile Island nuclear accident. Only France and Japan seriously persevered, and each for their own particular historical, strategic and security reasons. This time around, the fall in oil prices has been accompanied by cheap and abundant gas as well as coal. Shale gas has effectively killed off new nuclear in the US. Coal and gas prices have driven down wholesale electricity prices across Europe. In Germany, Fukushima accelerated its exit from nuclear, but the economics of new nuclear have in any case been radically changed, from an assumption of rising prices to a world of falling prices.

As recently as 2014, the British government forecast

that the wholesale electricity price would keep on rising throughout the next decade. Thus, when the first of a planned new set of nuclear power stations comes on stream, it would be competitive against the assumed higher wholesale electricity price.

The developers of Hinckley, the first project, were therefore awarded a thirty-five-year contract at ninety-two-pounds per MWh (a megawatt hour is 1000 kilowatt hours) safe in the assumption that there would be no subsidy.

It is however, already apparent that forty-pounds per MWh may be a better benchmark and there are good reasons to expect low marginal cost renewables to drive it even lower later in the 2020s.

Current generation renewables and nuclear are therefore likely to be out of the market for a sustained period, and hence the subsidies that were supposed to wither away after 2020 are likely to be permanent. To be cost competitive, something more is needed on the technological side to bridge the gap with fossil fuel prices.

We are led to believe that the world's fossil fuel resources are finite and known, and that the peak of production has either been already met or will come soon. Gas, it is assumed, will follow oil. Put simply, we are going to run out of fossil fuels, and they will therefore get (much) more expensive.

For the peak oil advocates, the convenient truth is that decarbonisation via renewables and nuclear is not only good for the climate, but sound economics too......

Almost all of this is nonsense – and some of it is dangerous nonsense. There is enough oil and gas (and coal too) to fry the planet several times over. The problem is there may be *too much* fossil fuel, not too little, and that fossil fuel prices might be too low, not too high.

The Earth's crust is riddled with fossil fuels. The issue is not whether there is a shortage of the stuff, but the costs of getting it out. Until recently, the sheer abundance of low-cost conventional oil in places like the Middle East has limited the incentives to find more, and in particular to go after unconventional sources. But technical change has been driven by necessity – and the revolution in shale gas (and now shale oil, too) has already been transformational in the US, one of the world's biggest energy markets."

(Author's comment: It is not dangerous nonsense and, in my opinion [as well as everyone else I have spoken to] the price of oil will escalate. Although barrel prices seesaw, it will gradually continue ever upwards. Unless a miracle occurs, renewable sources will fail to match both the escalation of the price and the decline of the oil).

*

These are extracts, not full reports, from the writings of Professor Dieter Helm, the Oxford don who has dinner with the oil magnates.

This book is a courtroom, and you are the jury (as all books about peak oil should be) and in a courtroom every voice should be heard. Dieter Helm CBE (Commander of the Order of the British Empire) is not a small player. He is a very large player, and his prediction of lower oil prices remaining eternally low, making fossil fuels very viable to use, but not quite so viable to sell, has so far been borne out, ('So Far') being the operative words. Like the jumper falling from a hundred floor skyscraper, on passing the fiftieth floor, "So far so good!"

In July 2018, the West Texas Intermediate (WTI) price of oil went from $50 a barrel to $60 then $70 then $80, and now is back to around $55 a barrel, with Brent Crude (BC) stabilising somewhere between the two.

At \$10 dollars a barrel to pump in Saudi Arabia and \$20 in Russia, the current sale price of around \$55 to \$60 (early 2019) still shows a profit (although it may be set to crash back to below \$50 a barrel). And, as he says, if you are chasing national debt by selling your oil, you need to sell more and more, so you pump more and more. But *so what*? He is effectively saying. If it runs out here, then you move there – and anyway the call now is for gas.

Furthermore, predictions on car use are that electric cars will become cheaper and more efficient. By 2035 it is estimated there will be 100 million electric cars, they will be charged wirelessly from car parking spaces and the centre of roads, and all the parts will be made on site by 3D printers, not carried by ships across the oceans of the world. This prediction is based, not on the vagaries of global warming, but on the air quality in major cities. The question to the jury – and you are the jury – 'who is right'?

You have heard previous experts tell you how dangerous the situation could become when the oil finally runs out (with cheap oil making the situation worse, not better). You have now heard sufficient to realise that there is another, very powerful, academic voice, an economist's voice, saying the complete opposite and disagreeing with everyone else presented in this book. His is the first of the four distinct voices from Chapter 1: *The most loudly and confidently spoken opinion.*

Will we really be able to transfer to renewables in sufficient quantity and sufficient time not to need the final oil in the ground? Can we actually leave the damned stuff where it is and move on? My God, I hope he is right. I really do. I want my kids and grandkids to have a bright future, not one in which they are scrabbling for food and clean water in a post-apocalyptic world reduced to poverty and crime because of lack of energy resources. And I'm sure you feel the same way.

Is he a voice in the wilderness? Is he swayed by the mega-wealthy corporate company he keeps? How many other experts feel this way? Well, you might be surprised to discover, quite a few, *but they are all economists and academics.* Dieter Helm is very much an academic, and he is also an economist (remember the dislike of economists voiced by earlier experts). He is not a hands-on oil man (working or retired); he has never had his hands covered in oil (champagne or brandy maybe, but never oil).

The people he calls peak oil advocates (other than a few writers who are simply reporting what others say – like me) are almost all oil men, or close observers who have had a direct contact with the coal face (so to speak).

I personally hope he is right. Because if he is, we can all slip out of the oil and gas age and into the renewable age, like a fireman down his polished pole. But I strongly suspect he has an income, an industry, and a shareholder's axe to grind.

Much of this is common sense. It's nowhere near rocket science and you certainly don't need to comprehend anything as complex as probability theory. The technicalities of the removal of oil from huge sponges of the stuff beneath the ground are manifold, and we need only touch on those. But the personalities involved, the politics involved, the lies, the deceits and the vast monies involved: these we can look at, these we can speculate about... And, to put not too fine a point on it...

If a bricklayer tells me the bricks he is using are of poor quality, I'm going to believe him. A brick looks like a brick to me. If an electrician tells me the switch sockets in my house are from China and nowhere near as good as the switch sockets from MK Ltd in Basildon, I'm going to believe him. A switch socket looks like a switch socket to me.

And there's the rub: If an oil man – a hands-on oil man – tells me that the oil is going to run out in shortly over thirty years, or considerably less, I believe him. And in my opinion so should you.

If an expert on the subject tells me that in Southeast Asia and sub-Saharan Africa, almost 1.5 billion people do not have electricity, I believe him (or her). If they then tell me India has 260 million households that are also not on the electrical grid, I believe it, because I have been there, and watched them cooking over cow dung and wood. This sounds like a form of renewable energy (and therefore climate-friendly), but cooking that way produces black carbon and methane, both of which make the planet hotter, aside from the carcinogenic smoke which fills the cookhouse.

Nigeria too, has eighty million people not connected to any kind of mains electricity. Needless to say, I have also been there, and am only too aware of their ambitious plans to extend the grid right across the country. WikiLeaks has also pointed out how Shell Oil has spies in every single Nigerian government department, and has people on the payroll in all areas of government life. It is represented, says, Celestine AkpoBari, of Social Action Nigeria, in every Nigerian ministry, and is more powerful than the government.

*

All these places and many more require mains electricity and are working towards that goal. At the moment solar will not do it – won't even come close (except perhaps in Saudi Arabia). Although a single home-type solar panel has been successfully marketed in Eastern Africa, particularly in Kenya, to charge a phone and give some kind of light, they all want mains electricity. Solar, to them is currently a stopgap: very much a stopgap.

Recently Greenpeace went to some lengths to 'solar up' an entire Indian village with the very latest available technology. The villagers however, were so disappointed they insisted on being placed on the grid instead, even though the grid is notoriously unreliable.

Which means the burning of more fossil fuels (probably coal), but possibly gas. Like I have said, you don't need to be a rocket scientist; you just need to look around you. Either the products they are burning will hasten the end of the fossil fuel age, or they will contribute to us being fried alive. Either option spells disaster.

The previously mentioned anthropologist, Joseph Tainter, has said in numerous ways and on numerous occasions,

> "Technological diversity is not going to save us, as it has in the past. If we don't reduce our dependency on fossil fuels, tackle inequality and find ways to stop elites from squabbling among themselves, things will not end well."

CHAPTER 10

"We must face the prospect of changing our basic ways of living. This change will either be made on our own initiative in a planned way, or forced on us with chaos and suffering by the inexorable laws of nature."

James Earl (Jimmy) Carter 39th President of the United States

We are aware that the oil and gas are running out and that there is very little technology waiting to fill this massive gap. But aside from that, the developed world is facing other major problems: problems equally damaging and equally **un-talked about**. Meaning (as quoted by Jimmy Carter), we all have to change our basic way of living. What does the current worldwide lack of respect, xenophobic political chaos, loss of any kind of old-time morality and integrity, actually entail?

There are numerous astonishing facts allied to just that problem that you will never hear aired on Fox News.

For example: a report entitled *Shorter Lives Poorer Health* was published in the US in 2013 by the Institute of Medicine and the US National Research Council, which showed that, people in the United States were dying younger and were generally sicker *than in any other developed country in the entire world.*

Despite the alarm it generated at the time, nothing has improved. In fact, things are much worse. The report identified that people under the age of seventy-five, of either sex, or any ethnic social or financial group, die younger and suffer more injuries and illness, than in any other wealthy democracy on earth.

Figures, published in 2017, show life expectancy in the US has fallen for the second year in a row. Government policies and poor living standards play a substantial part, as does a massive increase in STDs, with Chlamydia, gonorrhoea, and syphilis leading an unprecedented uphill charge, along with the worst drug abuse epidemic in American history.

 This long-term public health crisis only began receiving the attention it should in 2017, since awareness has arisen that the report is not talking about bunches of 'turn on drop out' hippy kids. It's talking about ordinary citizens taking accidental or deliberate overdoses of opioids, and that this is now the leading cause of a non-disease type death for people aged from twenty-five to sixty-four in the United States.

Michael Botticelli, director of the Grayken Centre for Addiction Medicine in Boston, Massachusetts and previous director of the White House Office of National Drug Control Policy (ONDCP) under President Barack Obama, has said, quite categorically,

> "Opioid deaths in the United States now exceed road traffic deaths. It's the highest level we have ever seen related to drug overdose deaths. It has surpassed the peak of HIV deaths and the peak of gun deaths. To say it is the defining health crisis of our time is no exaggeration."

The principal opioid sold in America is a product called fentanyl. This is a synthetic opioid similar to heroin, but probably fifty to a hundred times more powerful, and a hundred times more dangerous. The endemic over-prescription of opioids began with a product called OxyContin that doctors were told to prescribe for severe pain: the initial purpose of the drug and the reason it was given a licence was for cancer patients only.

The outcome was that, from 2002 to 2010, because of deliberately misleading advertising and what amounted to the bribery of doctors, the drug took off like a rocket and quadrupled the amount of people dependent on what was a powerful addictive substance.

The pharmaceutical company Purdue Pharma makes a number of drugs intended for the relief of severe pain. But these drugs, such as MS Contin and especially OxyContin, were soon being used by addicts to crush, snort, chew, or inject the dissolved product. Any of these methods produces a significant risk to the abuser and can result in overdose and death.

Nevertheless, addicts used every known method to obtain the drug, including 'doctor shopping' to obtain as many prescriptions as possible. But even among conventional, non-addicted patients a huge risk of physical dependency develops. Cancer patients are different, and a strong analgesic opioid is indispensable to patients experiencing severe pain. But the stuff wasn't exclusively being pushed to cancer patients – because there is little financial gain in only acquiring cancer patients.

OxyContin became a hugely successful drug, ensuring that Purdue increased its return on sales from a few billion dollars in 2007, to $31 billion in 2016, and $35 billion in 2017.

The company pled guilty in 2007 to fraud; specifically, to using misleading advertising and promotional activity, and agreed to pay $600 million, the largest settlement for pharmaceutical misdeeds in American history. The company's president, the former Chief Medical Officer, and its principal lawyer, pled guilty as separate individuals to serious misbranding, and paid a total of $34.5 million in fines. Three top executives were also charged with a felony and received a sentence of 400 hours community service in drug treatment clinics.

Other cities and even states followed suit, and in 2007 the company was sued by the State of Kentucky. The company settled for $24 million. Again in 2017 it was sued by the city of Everett in the state of Washington. The case is still ongoing.

But Purdue was not alone. North Carolina has sued the company Insys Therapeutics Incorporated, for illegally promoting a powerful opioid based on fentanyl (again), called Subsys, and doing so during the height of the opioid epidemic. The lawsuit was brought following charges against several former employees who were caught successfully bribing doctors to prescribe Subsys for painful conditions *other than cancer*. Both these companies were the hottest products on Wall Street, with Subsys achieving a stock appreciation of over 700 percent.

In 2008 a company called Cephalon, which made fentanyl lollipops called Actiq, faced claims that company executives had overstated the claims for a drug aimed at treating Lou Gehrig's disease. Furthermore, the Federal Trade Commission claimed that the company had deliberately postponed the availability of a generic version of a drug called modafinil (Provigil is its brand name).

In 2008 Cephalon settled whistleblower lawsuits amounting to $425 million paid to the federal government, including a criminal charge alleging the company had marketed the products Actiq, Gabitril and Provigil for unapproved uses.

This problem does not just exist in America (or in American companies). The UK has a serious and equally unrecognised problem with fentanyl and oxycodone. In January 2018 Public Health England launched a review into the growing problem of prescription drug addiction in the UK. Drug overdoses in 2017 hit record levels in England, Scotland, Wales, and Northern Ireland, sparking fierce criticism of the government's approach to drugs and addiction services.

Recent MSN news postings by David Cohen, of the *Evening Standard*, outlined the 'Opioid Timebomb' in Britain, by describing the financial and social collapse of a business man earning

£150,000 a year. This gentleman wanted to point out to everyone that, because of his unexpected addiction to prescription opioids, which he was obtaining both from a drug dealer and from the internet, he ruined his own life.

He was, he said to David Cohen, hooked in only two weeks. The married father of five children lived in a £750.000 barn conversion, drove a Mercedes, and sent his children to private schools, all due to a successful building surveyor business he ran in London.

He described how he met his dealer every fortnight in Oxford Street and handed over, in broad daylight, £500 for oxycodone (in street speak, 'oxy'), until he was consuming 200 milligrams a day. Oxycodone and fentanyl are currently responsible for over 17,000 deaths in the US. They were used, in his case, he said, to alleviate stress.

He also described how quickly he became hooked, and how impossibly ill he felt if he tried to stop. He thought to himself: 'They are given out every day by doctors, how bad can they really be?' Eventually he tried Googling for the drugs, and a dozen sites came up.

Eventually his entire world fell apart. In short order he lost his business, his wife, his children, and of course his dignity: he now lives as a lodger in a shared east London bedsit. He says he wants to send a wakeup call to the government. These things, he says, take a flamethrower to your life, and he wants as many people as possible to know that. (I have deliberately not mentioned his name.)

We are not talking here about what the British police call 'county line dealing', where youngsters as young as ten, or twelve, are used to package and sell opiates of various kinds across county lines to confirmed addicts. We are talking about prescription drugs and adults who were never previously addicts.

Deaths involving poisoning by opiates, cocaine, and amphetamines, including MDMA, have all reached peak levels, according to a count of coroners' rulings recorded in the UK in 2015. Similar data has been collected by the Office for National Statistics (ONS) which gave a level of drug-related deaths in 2016 as being 4,611.In the United States, 2,800 deaths a month occur from accidental overdoses of prescription opioids. We are also failing to follow the evidence to any kind of logical conclusion.

Although he had been arrested and imprisoned twice before and twice escaped, Joaquin Archivaldo Guzman Loera (El Chapo), was finally extradited via an aircraft to the USA, to face the criminal charge of leading the Mexican Sinaloa Cartel, the largest illegal drug dealing empire the world has ever seen. Millions upon millions have suffered because of him and his widespread trafficking in the drug fentanyl, which his cartel either cut with heroin (making the heroin much stronger) or sold as is.

*

The possibility exists that the entire American and/or British drug problem could have been stopped in its tracks, or at least seriously alleviated, many years ago, by the use of another drug named ibogaine.

CIA research into psychedelic drugs, instigated by Nazi scientists brought to the US during Operation Paperclip, investigated brain-washing and mind-control techniques during a secret 1953 programme called MK-ULTRA. During this research they inadvertently discovered that the drug ibogaine could instigate a thirty-six-hour intensive psychedelic vision, similar to the most intense religious experiences of historical mystics.

After this experience nobody wanted to be a drug addict of any kind, even if they were previously hooked on the strongest heroin, cocaine, alcohol, cigarettes, or any habit-forming substance. After taking the drug themselves, over 50 percent of the CIA agents involved, handed in their notices, much to the consternation of Allen Dulles, the then head of the CIA.

This astonishing drug has an illegal status and has since disappeared into history. But its social advantages were immediately recognised by Mary Pinchot Meyer, the wife of a top CIA agent named Cord Meyer. Mary, who was one of the (alluded too) mistresses of President John F. Kennedy, collaborated with the psychologist and writer Timothy Leary, in a somewhat naïve attempt to instigate world peace and a reduction in the drug problem facing America, by using both LSD and ibogaine to control crime and all other forms of drug abuse.

Once they realised the consequences, this did not sit well with the illegal or the legal drug cartels, including the breweries and the cigarette companies. While out walking along the Chesapeake and Ohio Canal towpath in Washington in October 1964, Mary was shot. The culprit was never found.

*

I have no time for any of these drug dealers; their God is money, and nothing else, and they all deserve their various punishments. But someone please tell me: what is the difference between a slime-ball like El Chapo, who will probably get life imprisonment, and drug companies pushing their junk in white coats via doctors and clinics, when they are well aware of the seriously addictive consequences, and consequently getting just as rich as El Chapo on the proceeds?

I'll tell you what the difference is... There is none!

*

In 2017 a report commissioned by President Trump made fifty-six recommendations for combating substance use, firstly by making treatments more available, and secondly, rather than sending people to prison, sending them to specialist drug courts that make suggestions about the correct approach and treatment available, plus supporting affected families. However, none of this has been implemented and no additional funds have been made available for treatment centres and prevention programs.

Trump also declared a public health emergency. This emergency period was to be of ninety days' duration. It expired on 23 January 2018, during this so-called emergency period, with nothing apparently achieved, although a renewal has recently been announced.

In an interview with CNN, former Democratic representative Patrick Kennedy referred to the above as, "Reshuffling decks chairs on the Titanic." Botticelli, ex-director of the White House Office of National Drug Control Policy, reiterated that, "We have seen White House posturing that would actually have a significant detrimental effect." The truth is, Trump talks the talk, but never walks the walk. And if that happens (with any president) during the demise of oil or the rise of global warming, then it's 'Goodnight Vienna' – and everywhere else too.

Trump promised to repeal the Affordable Care Act (ACA), implemented in 2010 to ensure affordable health insurance – hence health care. The policy has been a lifeline to people dependent on opioids. It is considered one of the ten essential health benefits that must be offered by all health insurers. Hillary Kunins, of the New York City Department of Health and Mental Hygiene, has said, "Without preservation of the Affordable Health Act it will be very hard to turn this epidemic around."

But who's listening? Not Trump obviously, who has reneged on all his promises except those few that directly appeal to his core voters (who he will pander to, even if it hurts America and the world) and therefore promote himself as their ungainly, half-baked knight in shining armour.

Said Trump, waving his arms in the air, as he announced the medical emergency facing Americans in October 2017,

"We are going to have really tough, really big, really great advertising, because, as Americans, we cannot allow this to continue."

But close scrutiny in Canada on the effects of such 'scare the pants off you' advertising, has indicated that they badly scare the non-users, but have no effect on the users. Canada now has a much more effective style of advertising that offers advice on where to go and how to seek treatment. They don't portray drug dependence as a crime or a moral failing either.

Adverts alone (whatever they indicate) are of course not enough. Canada has centres that offer addicts a supervised and safe place to take their drugs, plus ensuring a large-scale distribution of naloxone, an overdose reversing drug, which can be administered by anybody after only ten minutes' training.

The US also continues to record higher rates of gun deaths and infant mortality than anywhere else in the world. According to the American organisation Gun Violence Archive, that collates statistics on gun violence, 65,310 people have been killed by guns in the last four years alone. Even as I write this, yet another mentally disturbed teenager has shot and killed seventeen of his peers. It will happen again: in a bar, in a club, in a restaurant, in a Mosque. The Second Amendment as currently interpreted is complete lunacy.

Astonishingly, the country spends a great deal of money on health care and social welfare – *a great deal of money* – equivalent to the richest countries on Earth. But it is so badly distributed and so badly thought through; it takes your breath away.

In 2016, the US spent $9,364 per individual, on healthcare compared to the United Kingdom which spent $4,094 per individual. And everyone in the UK can obtain free healthcare – *everyone!* You may sometimes have to wait a while, or occasionally hang about in an ambulance, but you will be seen and treated, completely *free*, to a very high standard, a standard only obtainable at the cost of entire houses in America.

(On a personal note: I have had hip replacements to both legs, caused initially by a sailing accident. It cost me a total of £3.75 in hospital car parking fees.)

The problem, according to the report, would seem to be limited political support among, not just the politicians and policy-makers, but also the public to enact a better organised distribution of health care at affordable prices. Plus, there are shocking hikes in drug costs due to takeover companies, such as Valiant, who target specific, but little-known pharmaceutical companies that supply rare, but desperately needed drugs. They then move the price from a few dollars to hundreds of dollars while doing virtually no R&D themselves.

The Wall Street wolves thought this technique an excellent business model, as they did with the other *drug dealing* companies. And there lies the root of all your problems: hiding like sociopathic ninjas within the complexities of all the rip-offs, plus the coming oil and gas problem, the Wall Street wolves and the City of London stock exchange.

Other sad foul-ups include the previously mentioned Affordable Health Care Act: although not perfect, in 2016 it provided millions with health insurance. The US Congress has repeatedly tried to repeal this act and aims to weaken it at any price (God only knows why). In the interim the Children's Health Insurance Programme (CHIP), which provides low-cost coverage to nine million children will go unfunded (*New Scientist,* 20 Jan, 2018, p24).

Polarisation of policy and politics are no excuse for any of this. The future in which the fossil fuel glut is curtailed through absolute necessity or its eventual non-existence and the resultant huge price rises of just about everything, is going to be bleak enough for all God's children, without the US trying to win the race by getting people used to utter misery as soon as possible.

CHAPTER 11

"Unlike my opponent, I will not let oil companies write this country's energy plan, or endanger our coastlines, or collect another $4 billion in corporate welfare from our taxpayers."

Barack Obama, 43rd and 44th President of the United States

Christianity in its multiplicity of forms is interesting, don't you think? Even world famous scientists like Steven Hawking, found it interesting. It's a concept, an idea, a faith, a symbol, an emotional and philosophical treatise as alarming and fascinating as dark energy, black-holes, anti-matter, quasars, the over-light Higgs boson, and the on-going search for extra-terrestrial intelligence. It's a whole enchilada: including a form of glue, a mental opiate, a deep-seated need, and of course, a conman's paradise. It's all those things and more.

In terms of glue, it's the adhesive that holds continents like Africa together. As an opiate it becomes the narcotic that millions adhere to in order to ease their emptiness, poverty, and pain. A religious belief system is rarely an intellectual decision. It is, of course, also very dangerous.

An example of that danger exists in America, where it's become a political football. Whether it's even vaguely true or not is beside the point. We are nevertheless fairly certain that it is historically accurate. *Or are we?* Many experts argue that a host of scriptural passages can be viewed with scholarly suspicion. Such as the last twelve verses of the Gospel of Mark, which they think were tacked on many years later, including Jesus' birth in Bethlehem at the beginning of the Gospel of Luke.

Furthermore the Roman cult of Mithras, which most scholars assume predates Christianity by 500 or 600 years, was celebrated on a Sunday. Its principal festival was held on December 25th. There is a death and a three-day resurrection. Mithra was often called the 'Messiah'. Scholars agree that it is clearly a redemption religion in which water plays a redeeming role. Many scholars therefore believe this to be the basic foundation of Christianity.

Nevertheless, the majority of such scholars agree that Jesus was a real individual who embarked on a three-year mission to promote his own (and some Essene) radical views of the Jewish religion and was executed. Religious scholar's doubt he was crucified in the manner depicted, because trees (of any kind) were in very short supply in Judea and the very *first* image of the crucifixion of Jesus occurred in the fourth century CE. Whether he was, as Christians believe, the son of God and rose from the dead, is a different story.

Rome, that voluble civilisation that loved to praise itself and its nefarious deeds, had nothing at all to say about Jesus during his life. But they do mention that during his ten-year rule, Pontius Pilate executed a staggering 300 messiahs at the request of the Sanhedrin. Decades later, Jesus is eventually mentioned by the Roman historian Flavius Josephus, and the Roman senator Tacitus. Both briefly described his execution, but only after Paul had managed to spread the Christian message (as he personally saw it) deep into Roman society.

But – and it's a big *but!* – The canonical gospels were *not* written by the disciples Mathew, Mark, Luke or John (whatever your

Christian friend or pastor says). Nevertheless, they were certainly written by someone (or some-few). No one can deny that the entire conglomeration has swept the world, occasioning love, empathy, concern and kindness, as well as extreme violence, hate, despair and a disheartening scientific ignorance. Like all human historicity and endeavours, it has more faults than my first car. But it's unquestionably here: and consequently a force to be reckoned with. Personally I advocate the mathematician and Einstein's best friend, Kurt Gödel's axiom: that God (or at least a universal control set) can be shown to mathematically exist, and hence, there might also exist an afterlife, but that such knowledge has little or no connection whatsoever, to any earth religion.

*

In 2017, former Alabama State Supreme Court Judge, Roy Moore beat to the punch the incumbent, Senator Luther Strange, who strange to say (pun intended) had the backing of Donald Trump in the Alabama Republican senate primary and the Republican Party in general. Moore is a firm believer. He even embraces Christian theocratic principles as the basis for a system of government. He has, in the past, referred to God as, "The only source of our law, liberty and government" and that, "the First Amendment does not apply to Muslims."

The First Amendment (for the sake of British readers) prevents the US Congress from making any law respecting an establishment of religion, prohibiting the free exercise of religion, or abridging the freedom of speech, the freedom of the press, the right to peaceably assemble, or to petition for a governmental redress of grievance. It was adopted on 15 December 1791, as one of the amendments that constitute the Bill of Rights. But Moore thinks there are no such rights for Muslims and that the wording of the First Amendment is based on the words of Jesus.

In the UK he would be considered certifiable (and I have a sneaky feeling in New York, too). He has also made clear to friends, family and associates that homosexuality should be a capital crime.

The Pew Research Centre conducted a poll in Alabama in which 82 percent of the residents of the state are absolutely certain that their version of God and the Holy Spirit exists and is accurate. Perhaps their God exists in Alabama, but not in Iraq, Afghanistan, South Sudan, or Syria. You're the jury – what do you think? Either way Moore's beliefs have led him to make clear that, "God's laws are always superior to man's laws."

And, as a government official, he intends to put that concept into practise. Any conflict of interest between his notion of God and the law of the land will favour his notion. It's a philosophy (or a mental condition) that he would have carried to Congress, had Doug Jones not won the special election in 2017 instead. He has already intimated that Muslim Americans should be prohibited from holding elected office, and, as a judge, he once, during a divorce case, used a lesbian's sexual orientation to justify denying her custody of her own children.

Do they breed them in the southern Unites States? Is there, *like* (as my daughter would say), a special area for fruitcakes?

Moore's first major public display of pique occurred in 1995, during a period in which he was a county judge. He hung a wooden plaque of the Ten Commandments behind his bench, and would only begin the court's proceedings after saying a prayer in the courtroom. The American Civil Liberties Union sued to have the plaque removed and stop the prayer ritual. But Moore refused to back down. According to the Southern Poverty Law Centre, the case was eventually dismissed.

He was also sued by three separate lawyers after erecting a large and heavy monument to the Ten Commandments in the state judicial building. The lawyers argued that the monument gave the impression that, if you did not believe in the Old Testament, the court would not allow (as the British army would say) 'your feet to touch the floor'. In 2002 a federal judge ruled the monument unconstitutional, but Moore ignored the judge and was subsequently removed from the bench.

The basis of Moore's beliefs, and others like him, is frankly not too dissimilar from the ultra-conservative Wahhabism of Saudi Arabia. He has been associated with Dominionism, a theocratic approach similar to Christian Reconstructionism. This concept was developed by the Calvinist theologian Rousas Rushdoony, in the late 1970s, and is one to which several Republicans (claim to) adhere.

It is the belief that America is, and always has been, a 'Christian' nation, and that it is the duty of 'Christians' to restore 'Christianity' to its original belief system, in which the legal system is based, not on the American Bill of Rights or the American Constitution, but on the laws of the Old Testament. Indeed, Moore believes the Constitution is only legitimate insofar as it reflects biblical principles. As Moore has said publicly,

> "The First Amendment was established on Christian principles, because it was Jesus that said: 'Render therefore unto Caesar the things which are Caesar's; and render unto God the things that are God's."

But for Moore, it seems, most things turn out to be God's. Incidentally, Moore has been accused of sexual misconduct with several teenage girls. Why I am not surprised?

*

What does any of this have to do with the loss of the oil and gas and the subsequent failure of a complex society to sustain itself? Quite a lot actually! The 'End Times' concept belongs to these people and we need to examine the relationship between the demise of oil and gas, and their view of *our* demise. Maybe we'll find a match. But maybe not!

So-called Christians have a slew of opinions about the end of the world, which are rooted in a variety of interpretations of the Bible, particularly the Book of Revelations. However, the belief in 'an end of time' and a subsequent 'rapture', in which believers will be transported to heaven, while non-believers and 'can't make up your minders', will be abandoned to their own devices, began with our own Puritan fundamentalists in the eighteenth century: particularly with Increase and Cotton Mather.

*

Increase Mather was born in Dorchester, Massachusetts Bay Colony, on 21 June 1639, to the Reverend Richard Mather and Katharine Holt Mather, who had arrived with the so-called Great Migration from England, due to beliefs that opposed those of the Church of England. He was the youngest of six brothers, three of whom also became ministers. Since those early days, the narratives surrounding the 'end times' and the so-called 'rapture', have become very much an American phenomenon. In fact, 59 percent of American Christians in the South and West believe the rapture will indeed take place.

Increase Mather's son, Cotton Mather, suffered from a debilitating stutter but was nonetheless a bright student who entered Harvard at twelve years of age and received his MA at eighteen. He was an advocate of inoculation for smallpox and had a scientific mindset. He was, however, also obsessed by mental images of Satan and his nefarious deeds, and although he initially showed interest in becoming a doctor, he became a preacher.

His interest in the craft and actions of Satan made him a seventeenth-century rock star, and he preached about the wiles of Satan, particularly as they affected the moral strictures of young attractive women, with a passion astonishing to behold. He was directly involved in the Salem witch trials and heavily influenced the opinions of the most powerful individuals involved in the trial proceedings.

Before the outbreak of accusations in Salem, Cotton Mather

had already published an account of the so-called *possession* of the Goodwin children of Boston. Mather took the eldest child, thirteen-year-old Martha, to his home and made a closer study of Satan's wiles. Psychologists have suggested that his book entitled *Remarkable Providences,* which was actually published in 1684, describes almost 'to a tee' the symptoms of clinical hysteria.

It was this same hysteria that provided the model for the later behaviour of the afflicted girls of Salem. This furthered Mather's notion that New England was a battleground with Satan as the adversary. He carried this theme into his children's books, in which he warned young readers of an everlasting burning and foretold that those who do not pray, God will surely destroy.

Scholars have suggested that Mather's dramatic and frankly ludicrous descriptions of the devil's actions upon the young Goodwin children led to the first cry of witchcraft amongst the young girls in Salem village, the final awful outcome of which we are all too aware.

He also caused the clergyman George Burroughs to be hanged, even though the minister recited flawlessly the Lord's Prayer, a feat which Mather had previously predicted could not be achieved by Satan. Mather, it seems, shouted to the divided, none-too-sympathetic-towards-him crowd witnessing the event, "The devil has often been transformed into an angel of light."

This is exactly the same seventeenth-century type of baloney that is bandied about by advocates of the 'rapture' and the subsequent end of time, in places like Alabama today. The technical term for the end-times scenario is eschatology, a term based on the Greek word *eschatos*, which means 'last'

There are various belief systems pertaining to eschatology. One is called Millennialism. In this traditional belief, Christ will rule the Earth for a period of a thousand years (millennium), and this will be a time in which everyone accepts Christ as the King. At the end of this time Christ will judge the living and the dead.

Modern millennialism does not stipulate any exact interval or time period but leaves the question open. The principle idea being that there will be a given period, during which God's will, shall be carried out on Earth. This is the most popular interpretation amongst Evangelicals, because it also suggests that the world will be turned on its head, and then be taken over by the meek, or the good and the righteous, and that this period will be a time of peace and justice.

It also implies a solution to the problem of evil in the world – as in, why God allows such evil to take place and go unpunished, by implying that at the end of time there will be justice for everyone. Evil, including past evil, will be punished and the good rewarded, as God finally balances the scales of justice at the end of time.

(Yes, I know you are the jury, but please: no negative comments, such as –*it's about perishing time*.)

Pre-millennialism is a doctrine particularly popular among Evangelical Protestants. Other pre-millennial groups include Jehovah's Witnesses, the Exclusive Brethren, and Seventh Day Adventists. It is often mocked as the belief that 'the end of the world is nigh'. Pre-millennialism states that things are getting steadily worse and will go on deteriorating until God has had enough and takes action in a way that will be catastrophic for humanity.

Well to be perfectly honest, that doesn't sound too far from the truth. Only it won't be down to God, or Allah, or Jesus, or even Mohammad. It will be down to humanity's own slow-minded stupidity, based on not foreseeing the results of the demise of oil and gas and what, in the meantime, it is doing to the world's climate. No other reason!

Pre-millennialists believe the second coming of Christ will happen at the start of the afore-mentioned thousand-year millennium, when Christ rules the world. However, before this millennium period starts, there will come a time of destruction, war, and disaster, on a grand scale, called the *tribulation*. This period ends by God defeating Satan at the battle of Armageddon.

Many (in fact the majority) of these people see the returning Christ as a sort of battle-hardened commander who leads an army to kill the evil ones. Some of Christ's early followers saw Jesus in the same light. Problem was: Jesus didn't see himself in that light. This doctrine is not endorsed at all by those Christians who see Jesus as a man of peace. Not some kind of latter-day George Patton on steroids.

Pre-millennial beliefs affect the way churches and their members behave. They believe that the important thing for Christians to do is to prepare themselves for the end-times and to convert as many people as possible into righteous believers ready for the day of judgement, rather than concentrate on deeds of kindness and humane social activism.

By cherry-picking certain Bible verses, they appear to actually want to hasten the end of the world because, they say, it's ordained (read the Bible again. It isn't). I honestly believe they would be far better off trying to convince everyone that alternatives to fossil fuels need to be addressed now. That rampant capitalism with only profit in mind should be seriously curtailed, and that simple kindness, not science-fiction-like beliefs, should dominate their thinking. Then maybe, *just maybe*, there won't be any end times

Their current belief system, which is apparently shared by some Republican Senators and a surprising percentage of the House of Representatives, is not much help to anyone, quite frankly. They see little point in Christians attempting to improve the world around them by any method of social reform, since God is about to clean the world of its faults by destroying much of it and then remaking it.

*

The concept of the 'rapture' proliferated in the US after the Civil War, via the religious ramblings of figures such as John Nelson Derby. He referred to it as dispensationalism, in which different epochs or periods emerged. Different groups (to this day) hold differing opinions about how many epochs there are meant to be, including the epoch of Law: the period or epoch between Moses and Christ.

The period of Grace, which extends from Christ until now, is considered to be another epoch. This is followed by the Kingdom, the epoch before the end of the world. It begins with the 'rapture', and continues through a period of turmoil and chaos at least one millennium long, ending with the second coming of Christ.

This theology includes a fulfilment of the Old Testament promise to the Jewish people that Jerusalem would be restored to them. There is some dissent amongst believers whether this occurs before or after the 'rapture'. The restoration of Jerusalem to the Jewish people is part of the sequence of events that shepherds in the end times.

That is why Trump's controversial decision to declare Jerusalem the capital of Israel was significant to these right-wing religious fruits. Maybe, instead of concerning themselves with floating into heaven, they should concern themselves with the practical problem of making the world a better place, particularly for people they regularly ignore right on their doorstep, such as those in Tuskegee, Alabama.

*

Tuskegee is a largely black and ethnic minority rural community, not yet quite recovered from the infamous Tuskegee syphilis study. In this study black men from the area were deliberately injected with syphilitic bacteria without their knowledge, in the pursuit of medical data that might help the white religious people of Alabama when they inadvertently and surreptitiously contracted syphilis (hallelujah).

These black/ethnic communities are entrenched in poverty. Many families haven't moved very far since their ancestors were emancipated from slavery. There is no hospital facility within a forty-minute drive and they couldn't afford the simplest treatment anyway.

US hospitals also carried out experiments for the Los Alamos nuclear laboratory by injecting plutonium into unsuspecting cancer patients, in an attempt to discover what constituted a safe dose of radiation for those scientists working on nuclear bombs.

In the past, in the UK, as well as in the US, doctors have injected unsuspecting people with malaria parasites, meningitis bacteria, polio virus, and live cancer cells. Children with diabetes have had their insulin withheld until they were comatose, after which samples of their kidneys and livers were taken for analysis (Fred Pearce, *New Scientist*, 10 February, 2018, p43).

The beliefs of these Evangelicals and the behaviour they foster in others, such as 'turning a blind eye' to the scenario described above I find utterly repellent. This dangerous fantasy effectively says – don't do anything – *don't even try.* Just mind your own business because God has ordained this free enterprise system by giving the same chance to everyone, and as believing Christians, we will be saved soon anyway and leave all these socialistic sinners behind.

This unrealistic, nonsensical, politico/religious lunacy is luckily not held by the vast majority of the world's Christians, who respect the example and the wishes of Jesus as portrayed in the King James the First Bible, as being concerned with altruism and love for others, wherever they are, whatever their colour, tribe, creed or differences.

Not an –'I'm okay jack, up yours', self-centred, discriminatory, science-fiction diatribe.

CHAPTER 12

"As the wealthiest nation on Earth the United States has a moral obligation to lead the fight against hunger and malnutrition and to partner with others."

Barack Obama, 43rd and 44th President of the United States

In the UK (rightly or wrongly) we loved this black president. But he forgot to say – *starting with our own country.* Because I have to tell you, you could travel a long, long way in the UK, even Western Europe, and never find pictures like those above, photographed by Steve Liss, and Brenda Kenneally. Yet these photos were taken in the wealthiest country in the world – and not too long ago either.

They are shocking and they are not staged. Neither Steve nor Brenda stage photographs. They respect the tradition of the famous *Time Magazine*. Steve Liss was actually a photographer at *Time Magazine* for twenty-five years, and these are only three out of hundreds of such photographs. They are shocking because on their doorstep lies wealth beyond reckoning, oil wealth beyond belief, and Christian church congregations by the several hundreds of coach loads.

But the American South with its crackpot organisations, such as: The 11th Hour Remnant Messenger, the John Birch Society or the Aryan Brotherhood of Texas, has no time for the truth. This is made clear by the following longish commentary by Wayne Madsen.

"Donald Trump continues to push his full-throttled assault on the free press by claiming any news report that is critical of him or his policies constitutes 'faked news.' Not content with re-writing current events to fit Trump's agenda, some of his ardent supporters are now pushing the meme of 'fake history' to discredit actual chronicles of past events in order to advance false or misleading historical claims, or *radical religious dogma.* Promoting fake history is not the same as researching alternate views of history. Historical research is a dynamic pursuit and newly-discovered documentation often results in acceptable revisionist views of historical events. However, revisionist views of history are different than fake history, the latter having no proof of supporting evidence, but merely unsubstantiated ramblings found on dodgy websites. Trump, however, in his repeated attacks on 'fake news,' has legitimized those who traffic in fake history.

Betsy DeVos, Trump's billionaire secretary of education, is encouraging taxpayer-funded voucher and charter schools to teach 'Christian history'. This curriculum includes discredited 'creationism' and the rejection of the scientific evolution of species. DeVos is more interested in America's public schools building 'God's Kingdom' than in promoting true education, a goal that can only exist in a secular environment free of religious dogma and sectarian indoctrination.

De Vos and the Republican Party's overall support for historical illiteracy are compounded by the offerings on what was once known as the History Channel. This eyesore of the vast wasteland known as cable television, now offers such mindless fare as 'Swamp People,' 'American Pickers,' 'Counting Cars,' and 'The Curse of Oak Island.'

Instead of accomplished historians being cited for their work, a charlatan like Bill O'Reilly can claim the mantle of historical 'expert' because he wrote a 'Killing Series' of pulp fiction novels masked as historical research on the assassinations of John F. Kennedy, Abraham Lincoln, and Jesus of Nazareth; the alleged assassination of General George Patton; and the attempted assassination of Ronald Reagan.

Conservative commentator Glenn Beck is another purveyor of fake history in his writings and Blaze Cable TV network blathering. After the Dark Ages, Europe emerged into the era of the Renaissance. The arts and the study of history flourished. Hopefully the United States will emerge from the dark age of Trump into a new renaissance where historical fact wins out over ludicrous claims based on ignorance and intolerance."

All I can say to Wayne is, Hear, Hear! This time you appear to have it spot on.

*

But we digress: and we mustn't digress too far, because the issue at stake is loss of the world's energy. But what, at the end of the day, *is* energy? Why is the energy from oil and gas and coal and turf and wood so important to us? Aside from the obvious use of keeping us warm, what does it do? How does it work?

Well, for a start, without it nothing would exist. It's possible to say a play has energy, or perhaps a painting, or a dance routine. Similarly, we could say a toddler or a puppy has energy. It's not incorrect to say any of those things. A painting can have enormous energy in the form of impress-ionistic or mystical energy.

But physicists or engineers use the word in a more practical way: to them energy is quantifiable and measurable in terms of watts, joules, calories, horsepower, etc. Yet the quintessence, the ethos, the true nature of energy is still as mysterious to them as it is to a poet or a painter. Therefore, physicists and engineers are obliged to describe energy by what it *does*, rather than what it *is*.

It is generally known as the 'ability to do work', to change matter, to affect the external world (the world outside of your head). You cannot hold a jar of energy or see its shape or colour. Nevertheless, energy exists and without energy in the universe we would not be here.

In 1850, Rudolph Clausius and William Thompson stated that, total energy is conserved and cannot be created or destroyed, only trans-formed. In modern terms we could think of nuclear to mechanical (a submarine) or chemical to electro-magnetic (a battery). This law became known as The First Law of Thermo-dynamics.

The Second Law of Thermodynamics describes how, when converting energy from one type to another (such as the examples above) some of that energy is lost or dissipated in heat, leading to entropy (but is still there somewhere in the universe).

This loss is difficult, if not impossible, to recover; some energy is always being lost in any mechanical or electrical activity. Eighteen years later, in 1868, Clausius coined the phrase 'The Law of Entropy' to describe how in an isolated system the entropy always increases over time. Entropy began with the so-called Big Bang at the beginning of the universe. It is a form of aging over time, a collapse or dissolution of order, a form of corrosion or running down, a disablement – a continuous energy loss leading to eventual chaos.

The outcome is that, in the universe's battle between order and chaos, chaos will eventually win over time. Try for example (as one does as a student) keeping an old banger on the road way past its bedtime, and watch entropy gradually wear you and the car down to one young and one old wreck. It takes a lot of effort, a lot of work, to keep chaos at bay.

This is also true of systems, such as countries, cities, continents and civilisation in general: in fact, the entire planetary ecosystem. This applies to any complex system, which is only ever a temporary island of order. Take away its energy and the growth of its complexity and entropy sets in: its state of order becomes a state of disorder, and it eventually expires.

Matter is also capable of storing energy through its chemical compounds and complexity (such as coal). The trapped energy can be released through other chemical processes such as combustion (lighting the coal) or, in the case of living animals, digestion. Materials that store energy are called *fuels*.

The Earth is a closed system. All its matter, all its ecosystems are subject to entropy, so it is continuously being degraded. Nothing stays the same; mountains crumble, glaciers melt. Virtually all the available energy on Earth comes, one way or another, from the Sun, although so-called 'smokers' in the deep ocean exist, where animals gather around jets of heat from the Earth's core.

The Sun is a nearly perfect sphere of hot plasma at the very centre of the solar system. It is 109 times larger than the Earth; its mass is 330,000 times larger and accounts for over 99 percent of the solar system's mass.

Its energy output is equal to 100 billion nuclear bombs exploding every second, but luckily the Earth is 93 million miles away and so receives only a fraction of that colossal output. Nevertheless, we are constantly bathed in 1,372 watts of sunlight energy per square metre.

That's more than 10,000 times the energy from fossil fuels, hydro power, renewable and nuclear energy combined. How to harness that free energy is the problem. Well, it's one of the problems. The other is that industrial capitalist systems rely on financial returns in a feedback-loop arrange-ment of manufacturing, sales and profit, allowing funds for further manufacture. How do you maintain this system in any free energy bureaucracy? *Perhaps you don't!*

Perhaps the time has come to realise industrial capitalism's limitations and its appalling history of deceit and criminality. Andy Coghlan, a *New Scientist* journalist has said, "We can no longer pretend that simply letting the market decide will lead to anything but disaster."

There may however, in the distant future, be some kind of a way, since a clever and saleable idea has surfaced in which a tissue-thin solar array is wrapped right around the rim of the Moon (perfectly possible even now).

The Moon receives 13,000 terawatts of sunlight every day. This huge volume of sunlight energy could be caught by the solar array, and then beamed down to Earth via microwave technology. It would be sufficient solar power to energise the entire planet, and could be either sold in lots or packets to maintain the status quo, or applied as a free energy solution in a world that has finally abandoned the profit motive as selfish, pointless, and self-defeating.

The proponents of this idea have estimated that it would cost some £500 billion: the amount the current oil and gas industry spends pumping the stuff to the surface every two years.

*

Some people think, quite erroneously, that industrial capitalism, even though the industries involved were relatively primitive, such as sword making and amphora production, began at the same time that democracy theoretically emerged in Athens in the fifth century BCE.

They couldn't be more wrong. Industrial capitalism began in England in 1760 and real democracy has its roots in the hunter-gatherer bands of *Homo erectus, Neanderthal* and early *Homo sapiens.* It was experimented with, to some minor extent, in Greece in the fifth century BCE and morphed gradually from the Greek and Roman versions into the British version. Even this version could not be qualified as a democracy until 'The Representation of the Peoples Act' of 1918 (after the First World War) which gave the vote to women over thirty, as long as they owned land or property, or were married to a man who owned land or property. Not until 1920 was the vote given to all men and women over twenty-one in America and not until as late as 1928 in the United Kingdom. A real democratic political system did not exist anywhere in the world until the 1920s.

Democracy is a direct, people-driven reaction against the concentration of power in an oligarchy, an all-powerful kingship situation, or an all-powerful, male-dominated politic (in which serfdom becomes the norm) because it implies that everyone should participate in decisions regarding the allocation of resources. Democracy is considered an inherently Leftist construct, notwithstanding the distinctly undemocratic nature of the countries in the previous Communist Bloc.

It is deemed by academia that the altruism reflected in group democratic decisions by early familial bands of fifty to a hundred humans was a natural process, part of the need to assimilate and protect. The later right-wing (or opposing) view within democracy (the free market concept in which it's okay for certain individuals to prosper at the expense of others) is more recent. It was adopted after the start of the Industrial Revolution and an emergence of both financial greed and a desire to emulate the previous social structure of class and birth superiority, particularly in the United Kingdom.

So, it's our fault again! Reagan, Bush, Trump, Blair, Thatcher and their like, are our fault. Can you believe that?

Whatever the case: the Leftist and the Rightist viewpoints appear to be something of a dynamic within every civilisation. Even though there are people still alive who were there when it truly flowered during the latter part of the First World War. But just watch what happens as the oil extraction peaks, and energy resources become scarce. We will witness a shift of the entire political landscape, as both the Right and the Left struggle to come to terms with their oversights and the new reality.

The Right will seek to exploit peoples' competitiveness and their inherent need for security and authority during times of upheaval and instability. The general public, seeing the wheels coming off the wagon, and fearing a breakdown of law and order, and further wanting to know who they should blame for mounting economic problems over which they have no control, will almost certainly rally around 'strong' leaders, who offer unfortunate scapegoats, and will attempt to instigate 'law and order' by whatever means necessary.

The Left will blame the Right, and vice versa of course, everywhere, from Germany to Poland, back to the USA and the UK. The Right will blame the previous oversights of the Left and then become entrenched in a bitter financial and physical fight for survival.

Since the Right in all countries (except for the Nazi Right) almost universally represents the factory-owning, share-owning, business class, they will receive the brunt of the blame from the Left and be accused of holding back renewable and alternative technologies in their eternally greedy concern for carbon profits and personal gain at any price. Even at the price of the planet.

In truth, I strongly suspect that most people will not be aware of the reasons why the wheels are coming off. Politicians will not admit their failings; they never do. Academics and business-oriented people will realise the country is running on fumes but it is unlikely politicians will admit that fact, either over the airways or in the newspapers. But the intellectuals, those in the know on both sides, will be outraged at their respective political leaders for not recognising the obviously inevitable energy transition and their failure to do anything about it.

If, out of this debacle, the Right gains the upper hand politically (particularly the looney right), the result will be the undermining of civil liberties, with increased imprisonment or containment. Lefties, all minorities, and foreigners will become scapegoats and an expansion of the police and the armed forces will follow. Democracy will become a sham – a joke. The poor will be swept aside, unable to compete or to cope. The suicide rate will soar.

If the Left gains the upper hand (the more likely outcome in the UK) a sort of peoples' revolt will take place, in which demonstrations will sweep the country and blame will be directed towards the economists, intellectuals, and the politicians. But again, little mention will be made of the depletion of energy sources being the true problem. Politicians will bend over backwards to disguise the real reasons for the changes engulfing society. It's extremely doubtful if the words 'peak oil', or peak anything, will be heard at all. The blame will always be directed elsewhere. The outcome will be arrests and violent confrontations; eventually law and order will break down completely and nobody will be entirely sure why.

*

However, another problem faces us before this problem emerges – or at least before it emerges with all guns blazing – and that problem is, of course, global warming. *Global warming* is not even a particularly dramatic term; nevertheless, the United States Department of Agriculture has decided to forbid its use.

The agency's director of soil health, Bianca Moebius-Clune, has said that, from now on the list of phrases to be avoided include 'climate change' and 'climate change adaptation'. They are to be replaced by 'weather extremes' and 'resilience to weather extremes'. Also banned is the expression 'reduce greenhouse gasses', which is to be replaced by 'increased nutrient use efficiency'.

I'm not kidding! The above is the absolute truth. Maybe her double-barrelled surname should be pronounced 'More-busy-Clown'.

The state of Florida has also forbidden its employees to use the term 'climate change' which, when accidently mentioned once in an important local government meeting, was only ever afterwards referred to as, "The issue you mentioned earlier."

As reported by *Politico* (an American political journalism agency), a supervisor at the Department of Energy's Office of International Climate and Clean Energy told their staff in no uncertain terms that the phrases 'climate change', 'emissions reduction', and 'Paris agreement' are not to be used in written memos, briefings, or any form of communication.

Presumably what you can't say can't hurt you. These are state level decisions arrived at by the use of policy laboratories, provided by the US federalist system.

The new governmental chief scientist appointed by Donald Trump is Samuel Clovis. Clovis is not a scientist of any kind, but was previously a right-wing radio host, who once famously commented that President Obama's voters were all 'Maoists'. He has also described global warming as 'junk science'. As a right-wing radio host he would, of course, know this for certain.

In 2012, according to Bill McKibben of the British newspaper *The Guardian*, the North Carolina General Assembly voted to prevent communities from planning or even discussing rising sea levels. Perhaps they should have enrolled help from King Canute, because the outcome was, as Canute discovered: none too successful. The legislation didn't work because Hurricane Mathew in 2016 drove a storm surge from the Atlantic into the Cape Fear River, creating damage estimated at almost $5 billion.

As McKibben has also pointed out, unprecedented coral bleaching, which is universally blamed on rising temperatures, destroyed vast swaths of Florida's reefs, from Key Biscayne to Fort Lauderdale. A survey found that two-thirds were dead or reduced to less than half of their live tissue.

Still, he says, it's possible that they might simply have needed to …increase their nutrient use efficiency.

Christopher Byrd, who was an attorney with the DEP's Office of General Counsel in Tallahassee from 2008 to 2013, has said,

> "We were instructed by our regional administrator that we were no longer allowed to use the terms 'global warming' or 'climate change' or even 'sea-level rise'. Sea-level rise was to be referred to as 'nuisance flooding'."

Not everyone agrees with human-made or human-aggravated global warming, even the occasional scientist, such as Dr S. Fred Singer who Trump listens to, but just about no one else agrees with: not in the international scientific community anyway. Singer has even suggested carrying on regardless with conventional coal-fired generating stations, making no attempt at all to capture the carbon dioxide, calling this type of technology a complete waste of money.

He believes the sea is not warming and not rising and satellite data decrees the atmosphere is not warming either, and that CO_2 is a good thing, not a bad thing. Every one of these opinions has been shown to be wrong – but he continues to stutter and stammer (he is very old) the same absurdities.

It's true that CO_2 makes things grow. But too much CO_2 becomes a greenhouse gas. It's also true the Bible says humans have dominion over the Earth, and many US Evangelicals take this as tantamount to permission from God to use nature as they see fit. (Actually, the Bible says, in The Book of Revelation, that God will destroy *those* who destroy the Earth).

Such an unbalanced Dominionist viewpoint conveniently ties in with the political agenda that opposes any kind of collectivism, so these people are always reticent concerning issues that need collective action. *But collective action is exactly what is needed.*

*

In December 2015, 195 nations sat at the Paris climate talks table and agreed to limit global warming to two degrees centigrade. That was a collective decision, a decision that made sense. At current rates of emissions, we have less than twenty years before such a rise is inevitable.

America was one of those 195 nations, but Trump, as we know, is backing out of it, even though since the Industrial Revolution global temperatures have risen by a single percent. To the uninitiated this rise doesn't sound like much. But in fact, it has already had a serious impact: not just at the small level, but at the very largest scales, such as melting glaciers in Greenland, and the Thwaites glacier in Antarctica, which are altering the distribution of water on Earth and nudging the planet's rotational axis, causing the North Pole to radically alter direction and head towards Britain instead of Canada. It has moved more than a metre since 2005, making the Earth spin marginally faster.

In the last twenty-five years Antarctica has lost 3 trillion tons of ice. This process is accelerating fast, and Antarctica is now losing ice at three times the rate it was before 2012, amounting currently to 241 billion tons per annum. If all the Antarctic ice melts it will raise sea levels by 190 feet; effectively drowning every major city on the planet (*Nature*, June 13, 2018).

Meanwhile in the UK, spring is beginning two weeks earlier than it did fifty years ago and autumn a week later. Many aquatic animals have shifted their stomping grounds hundreds of miles towards the poles (Fiona MacDonald. www. Science Alert.com).

Nights are also warming faster than days. Night is normally the period in which the planet allows heat to dissipate back into space; however, the extra greenhouse gasses are trapping ever more daytime heat at night. This becomes very uncomfortable during heat waves. If our bodies can't cool down at night it becomes harder to cope with the daytime heat. Storms are also becoming more prevalent and more extreme. The Europe-wide heat wave that struck in 2003 killed more than 70,000 people, mostly elderly and young children who are less able to regulate their core temperature. A study in 2004 estimated that the risk of such heat waves occurring in future has doubled.

Rain too is a serious problem. It has of course always rained, and us Brits are used to being rained on. But the rains of late are causing widespread flooding not seen on quite this scale before. Computer models show that a hotter atmosphere can hold more moisture; consequently, storms become more violent because of the extra energy available.

Satellite observations indicate CO_2 levels have made much of the world's desert areas greener in a short space of time, and flowers are growing in jungles they never grew in before. Sounds okay! As Dr Singer, the American global warming denier, who believes stalagmite evidence shows coronal ejections from the Sun is causing the excessive warming, has many times commented – *but it is not okay.* In Australia the extra vegetation is sucking up far more water and reducing river flows by as much as a third of their normal flow. The Nile too has greatly reduced its flow. NASA scientists, monitoring numerous satellites looking down at the weather from space, have totally discounted the possibility of global warming being caused by the Sun and are 100 percent certain it is caused by manmade CO_2 emissions.

Currently we are emitting over 38 billion gigatons of CO_2 every year and the world's energy demand is growing ever faster. The cutting back cannot keep pace with the growing demand. Even if we switch to electric cars in time and ocean-going ships come up with some means of combating their unbelievable pollution output, particularly that of cruise ships which are notorious CO_2 emitters and the cause of 40 percent of the extreme air pollution in Mediterranean coastal towns ... that still leaves aircraft (*New Scientist* 26 January 2019, p6).

Powering aircraft is no joke. It's recognised as one of the principal problem and will require the large-scale development of a renewable, sustainable jet fuel, which in the US alone amounts to 90 million litres annually. We have already seen that hydrogen could, theoretically, play step-dad: but only if the available technology allied to some radical new designs and brand-new technologies took off like a moon rocket.

But will it? You're the jury: what do you think?

Currently 150 billion pounds worth of jet fuel is consumed every single year. The consensus of most scientists, particularly European scientists, is that this is literally skin-of-the-teeth stuff. We will have to wean ourselves off fossil fuels pretty damn quick, or we are going to have to devise methods of sucking CO_2 out of the atmosphere on an industrial scale. Assuming the worst – that in the interim little changes, and we continue as we are now – 600 metric gigatons will have to be removed this century. It is estimated by academics that CO_2 emissions will have to be completely zero by 2070 to prevent climate disaster. Do you honestly feel either of those is likely: considering the perverse thinking in the current US, UK, Australian, European Union, administrations?

To stay below two degrees of warming by relying on planting crops to offset the use of fossil fuels, it is estimated would take 500 million hectares of arable land. That's a third of the world's crop growing area, equal to almost exactly half of the United States. As indicated in a previous chapter – *a totally unviable proposition.*

To stay below, *or even on*, the infamous two degrees, we need a radical change in mentality and thinking processes everywhere, and not just the bohemian, Greenpeace, happy-hippy approach either. We need Church leaders, politicians, business men, fossil fuel executives, bankers, solicitors, and corporate organisations everywhere: including the Mafia (assuming they want to exist into the future) and including, MI5, SIS, Cheltenham, the Home Office, the Ministry of Defence (MOD). And every other nefarious bunch of government agencies to take note of global warming and put their thinking caps on.

Entire nations need to make global warming their top priority with a consistent and rapid transfer to renewables, because our present course is set to take us to almost four degrees of warming. Even if the promises previously made in Paris are kept by every single country, which frankly has yet to materialise, we will see a rise of three degrees.

You are aware of what one degree has accomplished; what do you think three degrees will do to the planet? Particularly if the Gulf Stream slows down or stops altogether: a complete stoppage is deemed unlikely, but slowing down is *not* thought to be unlikely, and no one knows what effect that would have on the climate or the marine life of the area. At least they didn't, until recently.

At nearly six nautical miles an hour the Gulf Stream splits and becomes the North Atlantic Current, heading relentlessly towards Europe. It carries a river of warm water which traditionally was thought to act like a sort of electric blanket, or an air conditioner for Europe flattening out our temperature peaks and troughs. It was considered to be the principal contributor to the moderate climate of northern Europe because it shifts vast amounts of water from the subtropics to the arctic. It is, as suggested, a river, approximately sixty-two miles wide, and from three thousand to four thousand feet deep.

However, that view is now thought to be the scientific equivalent of an urban legend, or an old wives' tale. Recent computer simulations in which the Gulf Stream was removed from the equation showed no temperature differentials at all, even though the UK is close to the 50th parallel which runs through Newfoundland and Labrador in Canada. So why do we not have polar bears and also freeze our nuggets off in winter, as they do?

Well, it seems the oceans do still play an important role in keeping Europe's winters mild, but it has apparently nothing to do with the Gulf Stream. The winds that blow southwest from the Atlantic onto mainland Europe carry air that is relatively warm. Even in the winter the enormous heat-carrying ability of water means the sea cools slower than the land and this moderates the temperature of the air above the surface of the sea. In the United States and Canada the prevailing winds are known as the 'polar easterlies' and they are dry and cold, having lost their heat to the thousands of kilometres of land surface they've already passed over.

However, it would seem not everybody agrees. An article in the *New Scientist* journal, 17 March, 2018, page 6, suggests that, part of the North Atlantic Current might well shut down, with quite devastating effects. Marilena Oltmanns, at the GEOMAR Helmholtz Centre for Ocean Research, in Kiel, Germany has said,

> "No one knows for sure what would happen in the event of such a shutdown, some people think it might spell the end of the North Atlantic's relatively mild climate."

Other experts predict a sea level rise of forty centimetres around Europe and eastern North America. Yet other models suggest a worsening of droughts in West Africa and even as far afield as South America. There is even an academic argument that a shutdown would be permanent, leaving the climate irreversibly changed.

However, Erick Galaasen, of Bergen University, Norway, points to evidence that convection has stopped in the past, yet the Atlantic Ocean recovered every time. For example, 8,400 years ago an enormous glacial lake in North America dumped 150,000 cubic kilometres of fresh water into the Atlantic. Circulation of the Gulf Stream was halted but started up again a hundred years later. Not long in ecological terms, but a substantial stretch of time in human terms.

But what if the sea becomes fresher from the billions of gallons of fresh water released from the previously mentioned gigantic Thwaites glacier in Antarctica, and the Jakobshavn and ZachariaeIsstrom Glaciers in Greenland? Climate researchers think they have now passed their tipping points, allowing unstoppable change to feed on itself.

If these three glaciers completely melted, that alone would make the sea rise another five to seven metres throughout the world, drowning all the current coastal cities and virtually all the Pacific Islands, plus overcoming sea barriers just about everywhere. The Atlantic current would then stop and it would be a great deal colder. Consequently 'Great Britain' would become considerably 'less great', shrinking to a much smaller European island. At the current rate of melt, the sea is estimated to rise at least a metre in this century, causing numerous international problems.

The Intergovernmental Panel on Climate Change (IPCC) has itself cautioned that key systems could be pushed beyond their tipping points if rapid warming cannot be controlled. In the opinion of Professor Timothy Lenton, the Chair in Climate Change/System Science at Exeter University in the UK,

> "The threshold was passed in 2007, when a sudden increase took place in the summer melt of arctic sea ice. The consequence of which, could be that, with less ice cover the ocean will absorb more heat and prevent a winter refreeze, locking down the system into perpetual decline. To date annual sea ice changes have not disturbed overall global ocean circulation, but the Atlantic leg has already weakened markedly."

The science journalist Fred Pearce has said that,

> "A new flip could lose us the Gulf Stream (which might or might not matter) and collapse the Asian and West African monsoons (which will definitely matter) affecting the

livelihoods of billions." (*Parenthetical comments are mine*)

There is plenty of past evidence to show that tipping points exist, the problem is that no one knows when the tipping points will occur. In Siberia and North America, millions of tons of methane are trapped in the permafrost; these areas are expected to release all of their methane within this century. Methane is a very potent greenhouse gas, and although it doesn't stay long in the atmosphere, enough of it could instigate a runaway warming situation. Such an occurrence would be unstoppable. It is escaping as I write, but not yet in sufficient amounts to identify whether this is a normal process or a new phenomenon.

Trump's cronies' reassurances that runaway change is not currently taking place and therefore the entire enchilada is a fabrication, is itself the worst kind of dangerous fabrication.

Fred Pearce has also pointed out that,

> "We certainly shouldn't be reassured by the apparent lack of runaway change. Experiments with biological and chemical systems show that they become sluggish when they approach tipping points. They also show that sometimes tipping points are passed without immediate impact" (*New Scientist*, 24 June, 2017, p31).

Information about global warming characteristics is not new. In 1861 John Tyndall, FRS, a prominent Irish physicist who was renowned for his ability to explain complex science in easily grasped lectures, discovered that the atoms of CO_2 vibrate when infrared photons (heat) bounce off the Earth and are absorbed by the CO_2 and released again, only to fly off in all directions, resulting in more heat being trapped in the atmosphere.

This is the greenhouse effect, a double-header that fosters life but can create havoc. Some CO_2 is absorbed by plants, some by the oceans and some stored in rocks. CO_2 has a life of thousands of years in the atmosphere, so every molecule we place into the sky continues to thicken blankets of the stuff. The University of Reading's professor of climate science, Edward Hawkins, has said,

> "If we want the temperature to fall, we will have to invent a way to remove CO_2 from the air on a huge scale. In the meantime we'll need to adapt to a warmer world."

Another Nobel Prize winner was the Swedish chemist Svante August Arrhenius. Amazingly, at the end of the nineteenth century, he predicted that atmospheric concentrations of carbon dioxide caused by the world's emerging oversized carbon footprint would eventually overwhelm us all, particularly if we stood around and did absolutely nothing about it. He also considered that the eventual ensuing release of the vast volumes of carbon, such as methane gas trapped in the Earth, particularly in the permafrost and in ice, including that trapped in the sea floor and in peat bogs – all caused by this same overheating – would undoubtedly create a chain reaction we may never be able to control.

This gentleman was born in 1859: the same year in which John Tyndall first described gas absorptions, or what we now call the Greenhouse Effect. What amazing forecasters – what incredible dual foresight! Pity that our politicians do not have the same foresight: we might not be in this mess now. But it also shows how, when politicos of all brands and beliefs do not listen to scientists, all hell can, and *is,* breaking loose!

Is anyone in the Trump camp listening? Because you need too!

*

For three years in a row, carbon emissions have stayed virtually flat, yet the world economy is growing. This gives us a modicum of hope. Twenty-one nations have noticed that emissions and economic growth are beginning to advantageously separate somewhat, including the US, the UK, France and Germany (no thanks to Trump).

Why is this?

Well for a start, coal is being used far less. Coal is a horrendously dirty fuel: without full carbon capture, you might as well start seeding the atmosphere with thermal blankets. However, even if it's being used less, at the time of this writing, it is still the principal fuel in China and India.

Although China has historically contributed very little to atmospheric CO_2, its current breakneck industrial growth means that an industrial area on the outskirts of Beijing, the size of Carmarthenshire in Wales, thrusts more CO_2 into the atmosphere every hour, than the entire United States does in a single day.

According to the on-line *Independent News*, air pollution in China kills 4,000 people every day. Yet China is producing renewables at the fastest rate on the planet, many times faster than the United States. The Chinese media also talks about the science of global warming and the problems of using fossil fuels every day on radio and TV. In many ways China is more democratic, and much more open to science (real science) than is the United States.

In the US (more than anywhere else) coal is (luckily for us) being pushed out by renewables and gas (but mostly gas). In the UK gas extraction peaked in 2000, and is running out very fast indeed. In India the construction of certain coal-fired generating stations has actually been abandoned. Nevertheless, without American leadership in fossil fuel reduction, these developing countries will simply use what they have – and India has coal sufficient to last several hundred years.

Renewables are very gradually winning the day with more efficient turbines and cleverer photovoltaic methods of capturing solar energy: in some countries wind and solar cost the same, or even slightly less to produce than the various fossil fuel methods of generating energy. According to the World Economic Forum this will extend to two-thirds of all countries over the next ten years. The American Environmental Defence Fund has made it clear that solar and wind powers are both creating jobs twelve times faster than the economy as a whole.

This is all good news: although other voices further back in this treatise have supposed (unless we get our skates on) that we are headed for total disaster. This is not, for *one moment,* meant to be a doom-laden, filled with 'Oh-my-God! We-are-all-going-to-die, and there's sod-all we can do about it' manuscript. In which feelings of powerlessness are the dominant emotion. This is already the modus-operandi of the Evangelicals: do nothing-at-all-about-anything. They even emotionally and politically attempt to hasten this catastrophic final roll of the dice. Such messages can be extremely paralysing. We don't want you paralysed: **we want you – like Bill and Melinda Gates – active.**

There *is* hope, if we act, as Leonardo DiCaprio says... **NOW!**

We must ignore the weird views of the current American establishment that insists it's all spin. Science is constant in its opinion that global warming is human made, certainly human contributed, and that we have to do something about it as expediently as possible.

All this stuff is calculable and has been run through computer simulations many times and, when you run the global warming numbers, they inevitably reach 4 degrees Celsius (or worse) if we do nothing.

Have you the least idea what that means? It's not rocket science.

You might ask: why isn't any of the above the answer? In which we do not have to do a great deal more technologically to ensure our future, other than simply keep going the way we're headed: but just a hell of lot faster? Because, virtually all of the above entails various methods of ensuring a continuous flow of mains electricity. This means if we can make cars, trucks, trains, tractors, combine harvesters etc., etc., run off batteries that are rechargeable from the mains, **and the mains itself is using solar** *or nuclear*, or any other form of non-fossil fuel energy, then the day might be saved.

But that day is a long way off. It will remain a long way off as long as fossil fuels are cheap and the United States' conscience continues to hide behind huge piles of fossil fuel money.

Neither does it help aircraft to fly, nor ships at sea to carry the world's goods across the oceans, because clearly, they cannot run off rechargeable batteries.

*

There is another factor, one we have merely touched on, that could stop all hydrocarbon production dead in its tracks. Cost of extraction.

Trillions and trillions of the world's finances are tied up in the extraction and sale of hydrocarbons. There are hundreds of thousands of people employed in the industry worldwide. There were over 4,295 crude-carrying oil tankers plying the seas in 2008. That was eleven years ago and there are even more now.

An unstoppable industry, you might think: too large to go belly-up. Except that it can, and will – when it becomes impossible to produce a profit. The current production cost of a barrel of shale oil ranges from as high as $95 down to $40 or so. The industry is extremely cautious in view of the losses incurred during the last major investment into shale oil in the early 1980s. And although shale oil production is back in the frame, it is still heavily subsidised. It has subsequently been stopped in Australia because of environmental issues, and is teetering on the edge of no longer being viable at a number of sites in the United States, because it is essential to the industry that oil from shale comes in below the cost of crude.

A possibility not given much consideration by anyone is that technological advances in renewable forms of energy *may* bring down their costs to a level below that of fossil fuels. Such additional supplies into the energy mix may eventually (in only a few years) bring down the price of *all* energy sources, particularly oil and gas. At this point they will stop making any kind of profit at all, and therefore stop producing, but long before the alternatives are internationally viable.

They are, after all, in business to make a profit. We do not deny that. They have shareholders: CEOs and executives with eye-watering annual salaries. They have equipment on land and at sea worth many billions that could only be sold for scrap.

This might sound like the ideal situation. After all, the handwriting is on the wall. If oil and gas companies cannot even cover their variable costs (those incurred in producing the oil and gas, not taking into account depreciation, repairs, etc.) and gas is down in selling price to $2, $3, or even $4 Mcf (one million cubic feet), not only is it not worthwhile exploring for new wells, there is little point in continuing to scrape the barrel in existing wells. Massive subsidies, larger than the current global subsidy of 6.5 percent of the world's GDP, might keep the boat afloat for a short period but eventually it will sink with all hands.

What then sport?

Well it depends on how quickly that day arrives, as against how easily fossil fuels could be seamlessly replaced. At the moment, were this to happen or the global subsidies removed, the world's economy would collapse, and all the disaster movies you've ever seen would be rolled into one. So, the subsidies will remain until a seamless transition is possible. But the current subsidies, vast as they are, may be nowhere near enough; they may have to increase tenfold.

And this could be why, on the very day I am writing this chapter, the Chinese are starting to gently apply the brake on development of renewable energies. Last week China was the hero. China was way ahead of the US in its valiant attempts to stop living under a cloud of never dissipating smog. And they have not stopped trying to alleviate the awful air conditions in a number of cities. But in general, it seems, they are pausing to take stock.

Destroying the fossil fuel industry in China would throw many thousands out of work and could upset the delicate balance of power, because any autocracy/oligarchy is always looking over its shoulder. This is a great pity, but is understandable. After all, it's obvious that America couldn't care less, and everyone can see that. (America must be a real cut throat place to be a climate scientist or, with the current administration, any kind of scientist.)

Consequently, because of the lack of world leadership, many countries have not yet lived up to their promises at the Paris agreement. Yet very few environmentalists think that 2 degrees was sufficiently robust in the first place, and that the only answer is stringent carbon taxes applied as soon as possible.

It may be telling that almost all the oil producing countries in the world are autocracies of one sort or another. This includes China, Iran, Kazakhstan, Laos, North Korea, Oman, Saudi Arabia, Turkmenistan, United Arab Emirates, Uzbekistan and Vietnam. Russia is also an oligarchy, one which makes bizarre rules, such as an individual person can protest without state permission (but groups above one cannot) and then inevitably arrests the singular individual who does.

*

By the end of the century the world will be three to four degrees warmer. In the UK this means more rain – lots more rain. It's bad enough now, but step out of your grave and take a walk about a hundred years from now and check out the flood defences. Make sure you have magical waders because you're going to need them.

This country will be a very different place. Your house might still be there, unless it was built on a flood plain, or in a previously often flooded area. But you will be amazed to see the size and the power of our rivers. No longer poetically meandering their way through green fields and small country towns, they will be boxed in like sewers with huge flood defences. The coast will be a different shape and equally fenced against the type of storms rarely witnessed at the beginning of the twenty-first century. The summers will be much warmer and much wetter and the winters far colder.

Step out two hundred years from now, and not only will your house be gone, many well-known sights will have completely disappeared. Public transport via monorails which go everywhere will be the way to travel, not independent boxes on wheels with one or two people inside. Motorways will be few and reserved for cargo carried by hydrogen powered mega-trucks emanating from a hub in the centre of the country, where now stands Meriden in Solihull.

The sea will be farmed, and not just for fish. Genetically modified algae will supply much of the renewable energy needed and be grown on vast algae farms, freeing up over 68 percent of much needed fresh water.

DNA modification, which started out only available to the rich earlier in the century, will be available to all, via upgraded CRISPR. Virtually all genetic diseases will have been eliminated and a form of eternal life will be possible for those who really want (or who can afford) it, based on real and electronic immortality.

Fields in the UK will be growing CRISPR technology genetically modified crops, as far as the eye can see. We will be completely separated from European culture and influence. Most of our trade will be with China and the separate North American state of California.

In America, the 'Second Amendment' will have been abolished a long time ago. Carrying arms that fire bullets will not be allowed by anybody under any circumstances. Not even by the police, who now carry a form of directed energy weapon developed by DARPA (Defence Advanced Research Projects Agency) that temporarily paralyses.

Intelligence will be enhanced at birth. Population controls will be in place and geo-engineering will have solved the worst excesses of climate change. Living in the UK will no longer be living in a shower cubicle even though the summers are wetter and hotter by turns. Short-term wars will have been fought over the rights to the Arctic and the Arctic Ocean. The longest lasted four years. No one won: there was a compromise.

At the start of the century electronic currency was thought to be the future but this did not happen and local currencies now thrive. Some American states have their own currencies, and all the European currencies are back. The internet has been curtailed and sexual material of all kinds removed and no longer allowed. Women have equitable rights in salaries and opportunities.

Nuclear fusion (in which atoms are fused rather than split) will be available around 2050 to 2065, but will not be up and running until the end of that century. Solar energy facilities will be very sophisticated compared to now and will be micro-waved from the Moon. Wind power will have lasted until the middle of the century, but no longer be considered feasible in view of the available energy sources.

We will be radio-wave-wired to computers, of one sort or another, to both enhance intelligence and immediately obtain information. Alzheimer's will no longer exist. Expect this among the wealthy by 2150. By 2275 A.I will have taken repetitive jobs completely out of the market everywhere. Most people in the developed world will be able to use machine augmentation for their brains and, by the end of the century, pretty much everyone else.

Except where deliberately artificially, maintained (Welsh, Gaelic, Sardinian, certain Native American languages), all languages will have morphed into three or four, such as, English, Spanish, possibly French and Mandarin. China will be the world's leading power and the US will have split into various autonomous nations.

We will have colonies on the Moon and Mars. We will have had two or three attempts to colonise Mars by the end of the century, but they all expired. Astronauts will be genetically modified by CRISPR technology to be more resistant to bone degradation and unhelpful cosmic rays. Close space tourism to the Moon will be commonplace. There will be hotels in orbit. Embryo implantation will finally exceed normal impregnation.

Animals that were destroyed through poaching, game hunting, and loss of habitat will be artificially re-created from specimens in zoos, also by CRISPR technology, allied too much better cloning techniques. Large tracts of the sea and of Africa and of Asia will be animal reserves paid for by the World Bank.

The Sahara will be watered by AI weather control and will be mostly green. It will have become an animal sanctuary. Poaching will entail a death sentence by lethal injection. By the middle of this century few animals remained and drastic measures had to be introduced, first paid for by China and then by the World Bank.

Nanobots (nanotechnology) will be inserted into the human body to repair damaged and cancerous cells without the need for chemotherapy and its awful side effects. Watching one's family members suffer will be a thing of the past, as these miniscule robots tear through the bloodstream administering aid as they go. Plus, 3D printing of human body parts and organs, such as the kidney and the heart will be commonplace (work has already begun on such bioprinting by Jennifer Lewis's team at Harvard University).

British start-up companies are already making very strong and waterproof construction materials out of compressed potato waste, mushroom roots, and grass cuttings. This is just the beginning of numerous ways in which future homes will be built from tough, sustainable, organic materials which are not based on wood, brick or concrete.

Marriages will no longer be for life, unless both parties require that to be the case. Normal marriage will be for ten years. Same-sex marriage will be considered normal in the Western hemisphere, but still looked at askance in the East.

The wars of attrition between the West and the world's fundamentalist Muslims will have ground to a halt by 2030, but be reinstated by 2050, finally expiring in 2060, when it emerges that an alien species, who can alter our understanding of reality, have been in our air-spaces for centuries and have made it clear that all of our human interpretations of God are inaccurate: affecting both Christians and Muslims.

The shock will be profound and felt world-wide, and will re-start the remote controlled 2050 wars, which will be so violent as to make the present Iraqi and Syrian conflicts look docile. Millions are killed by autonomous machines and multiple millions maimed. The acceptance has still not entirely sunk in over a century later. Most churches, mosques, cathedrals and temples, have been demolished, or are now empty.

I'm guessing of course. But rather some, or all of the above, than a future that looks more like the bleak movie, *The Road.* And even if there are no wars, to arrive at the place described above, either a God-given miracle has occurred, or millions have died in the achievement from starvation, cold, heat, floods, and suicide.

Remember, you are the jury.

Will renewables control our future energy needs before either the oil or gas run out, or are too expensive to obtain? **They must.** We cannot sit on our hands and hope that is the case. We have to *make* it the case. Will the world come to its senses about global warming, those two obscene words you are not supposed to utter, especially in the United States – which is in a state of denial – because it must? Will a kinder, fairer, more beneficent political system develop – one which is less concerned with money and greed and naked power – because it also must?

So: talk about this book, lend it, discuss it, criticise it – send it to politicians. I don't care. But don't expect Westminster and the City, or the White House and Wall Street to satisfy the needs of the future, because they can't, and they won't.

It's *your* kids' future remember, and that of their kids' and all the kids' after them. Don't depend overmuch on politicians or big business. Depend on yourself. What happens in the next decade will reverberate down the centuries. We are on the cusp of great changes. No one likes change, especially changes which are life threatening, but they are right upon us, whether we like it or not.

*

Depending on one's self: what does that mean in practical terms? How can one take action to mould the world towards a more positive, rather than a totally disastrous, future? Let us consider what can be actually done.

Well, because the oil problem is considered a non-problem in the minds of governments and populations at large, a street-type protest, such as those by Americans wanting to change the ludicrous Second Amendment, would achieve nothing. In fact, so far, it has transpired that the huge protests following Trump's inauguration: the women's march on Washington: the protests following the Washington school shooting: the prolonged stand-off during the Native Americans' attempts to halt the tar-sands pipeline, etc., etc., all have come to nothing. Unlike France, America routinely ignores its protesters.

Beside which, protests of that nature will not emerge until the oil price skyrockets and petrol and diesel with it, followed by food prices and public transport costs. By then of course, if the alternatives are not in place, it's too late.

So, what does one do about any of this?

Outside of the ballot box – which hopefully will get rid of at least some of this current lunacy – write about it! Write to 'Trump the Wall', 'Trump the Chump', and ask him what happens when the oil and gas runs out? Quote to him the opinions of oil experts who are hands-on oil experts, not economists. Tell him we have thirty-five years or less (some predictions are as low as ten years). Write to the minister for energy (in the UK, it's the Right Honourable Gregory Clerk, as Secretary of State for Business, Energy, and Industrial Strategy).Send him this book.

Get together with others and bring lawsuits. Litigate against the governments and the various departments concerned with climate denial. Sue them relentlessly, and keep doing it.

In the United States, it's The Department of Energy, James W. Forrestal Building, Independence Avenue, Southwest, Washington DC: also, in Germantown, Maryland. I wouldn't, in this case, send them a book: you might receive an unwelcome visit from the FBI (or worse).

Write to your local paper; tell them you have read that oil and gas have a finite life much shorter than previous predictions, and what exactly is being done about it that makes any sense (and is in time)?

In fact, protest by writing to everyone you can think of. Or send them a copy and hope for the best. Don't bother to join the street protests when fuel prices go sky-high because by then it's much too late. If you don't already own some, you could perhaps buy some roller skates and start, like preppers, stockpiling tinned food.

One final thought by Baudelaire: "*The finest trick of the devil is to convince you he doesn't exist.*" I can assure you he does. His name is *not* Beelzebub. It's plain old-fashioned, unconcerned, closed-minded ignorance. Be aware of its existence!

Tell me how you got on at briannoble12@yahoo.co.uk. And, or, if you agree with much of this, say so on the Amazon book page.

"The fault, dear Brutus, is not in our stars, but in ourselves."

-     Julius Caesar

www.ingramcontent.com/pod-product-compliance
Lightning Source LLC
Chambersburg PA
CBHW070757240726
48654CB00007B/106